FROM NOWHERE
TO SOMEWHERE

FROM NOWHERE TO SOMEWHERE

An Uncharted Destiny

DR. K P MOKHOBO

To order additional copies of this book, contact:
Xlibris Corporation
0-800-644-6988
www.xlibrispublishing.co.uk
Orders@xlibrispublishing.co.uk
306231

CONTENTS

INTRODUCTION

The story is that of a success that could never have been anticipated nor be assured of achievement by some wilful manipulations of circumstances so amenable. The birth circumstances for a black baby borne on a farm remote from whatever health facilities there could have (though highly unlikely) been were primitive. The infancy to early childhood years are traced up to the stage where the piccanin or kaffertjie finds himself as a person. Throughout the formative years, under a variety of environmental and human sourced influences, my life path is one that is remarkable for how unintended events changed the eventual future completely. The progression to the SOMEWHERE, at all stages, seemed to have been by pure chance, whether such an event was some tragedy or death or some inexplicable happening. This chance road of destiny characterised even the school years, up to the miraculous entry to university and the subsequent professional journey. One of the noticeable threads throughout was the frequent spontaneous development of interpersonal relationships with strangers, friends and relatives, all contributing positively to my lucky breaks. My name itself, Kubedi Patrick, seems to have added the unforeseen attachment to the church forever. I was named after a local pastor of the AME CHURCH, Rev. Patrick Kubedi. There is throughout a wide circle of non-biological parenthoods that took charge of my prosperous upbringing, providing shelter, food and inspiration and nurtured many of my individual make up. I do not know what role my genes played. I underwent many adoptions by many different people, as well as "near adoptions" by those who took a liking to this "orphan" of nature rather too readily! I regard myself as total freak, with no permanent first level home or parentage, no organised life programme or future planned for, yet I managed to climb the socio-cultural-medical ladder without any difficulties or impediments.

THE ORIGINS

Mokhobo's mother with first two kids by first wife,

My baptismal certificate shows that I was born the fifth of July 1932, baptised the sixteenth of April 1933 by Rev P L Selepe, in the AME Church, district Bothavile, Free State. The "parents" or "guardians" are a Johannes Mokhobo and Lesitia Mokhobo. The former, I do not know. The latter, I guess is a misspelling of my mother's name, Lydia. This is pure guess work. Church practice is fairly liberal on the question of legal parents/responsible guardians in good standing. For the first ten to 15 years of my life, little direct information was given to me about my parentage. Somehow, I also, did not ask many questions, I guess because I did not" miss the role" of biological parents. I was comfortable with "what I had". As far as I was concerned, I enjoyed a complete childhood life like everyone around. I came to know that my mother was a domestic servant somewhere in Johannesburg, whom I subsequently "met "for the first time when I was already eighteen years old, by which stage I had acquired the ability to be fully independent and was on the road to being a self made person.

The story of my birth is that I was borne "out of wedlock", at Haaskraal, a farm outside Potchefstroom, towards the Free State border. By cultural language, I was a grandparents child (ngwana wa ko gae). It was alleged that my biological father was one Rantjapedi Johannes Motsemme, a person on whom I never laid my eyes. I subsequently met and lived with my older brother (1925-1965), who was a cripple. This story follows later, at Mooibank, a small farm ten kilometres from Potchefstroom town, where I returned home to my grandfather. My brother either had had poliomyelitis or some disorder that made his one leg shrivelled. I was also told of an older sister, Tlaleng, who apparently died in childhood. So I am the third and last child of Lydia.

Mokhobo's mother in the middle with church friends,
A M E Church uniform.

The traditional midwife who delivered my mother and named me after her father, was Jacobeth Kubedi. She herself never married and had only one child, a son Rev Moses Kubedi of the AME Church. My instincts right away, informed me that my mother would not be comfortable to talk about whoever fathered me or "us (brother David and/or sister Tlaleng). I must say that my brother and I looked no where alike, although this may mean nothing. My mother, also never volunteered anything about my paternal side and I left things as they were because I missed nothing in this regard. There was not even a spark of some curiosity to know. I cannot explain this, especially when one hears of stories or have read about and even seen films about grown up children being literally neurotic about searching for some unknown biological parent. Very late, when I was married with children and was a qualified doctor living in Mafeking (now Mahikeng), did I yield to pressure from uncles and aunts (Mokhobo side) to know my father. With the help of some grandmother, we went to Kgotsong Location in Bothaville. Unfortunately ntate Motsemme had already died. I was shown his simple grave and got introduced to his sisters, their children, two of his children by his other wife (also deceased) and many relatives. I obviously would not expect or be expected to bond in how thin a manner with any of these people. So, my mother proper in my first ten years of life was my mother's younger sister, Martha, married to Phanuel Mokobokoa Mpitse. It was said I was given to her for adoption by my maternal grandfather as she was thought to be barren. I believe I was two years old when the Mpitses took me from Potchefstroom. My arrival in the adopted home, indeed seemed to do the trick, the expected! My mmangwane (mother's sister) conceived and was blessed with a baby boy, Leepo Shadrack Mpitse. His grandparents, Tempese and Mmamokati Mpitse enjoyed temporary happiness, as Leepo's father was shortly after killed by lightning stroke, allegedly bewitched by one jealous Molelekoa. My stepfather, Phanuel, was liked by the farm owner, Mnr Von Abo, who made him a foreman and Mokobokoa was the only one able to drive a tractor in those days (Source of jealousy, including Molelekoa's). My stepfather died when I was eight years old, and Leepo two years old.

Mnr Von Abo had established a primary school at one of his farms, at a place called Smaldeel, towards Kroonstad. It taught up to standard two (four years of schooling). This is where I started school at the late age of ten tears. The reason was that the farm owner liked me and chose me from among other piccanins or kaffertjies, as we were called. I was assigned an important job to keep his younger son, Crawford Company until he was ready for school at the age of six years. I had a wonderful time "bringing" up young Crawford, most of all I enjoyed disposing of the food remaining after the family had eaten as this was nourishing and I believe gave me a balanced diet which offset malnutrition. The food at home was porridge with salt, sometimes sour milk or whey (karing melk). The farmer also reared milk cows and produced butter from cream. Meat was a rare delicacy on some Sundays or when some animal had died. The farm dwellers also would hunt or catch wild rabbits or other eatable striped mongoose.

I would also go out on other chores expected of all black children. This, in fact, became regular after Crawford had gone to school. Every winter for three months, the school would close and all, adults and children would go harvest mealies by hand and travel from farm to farm with the machine that produced the corn (off the mealie cobs).

Starting School

I did Sub A+ Sub B in one year by promotion 1942, as well as the following year, 1943, I completed Standard one and two. I credit my grandmother and midwife for delivering me without any mishap, whether physical or intellectual disability. It then turned out that the death of Phanuel Mpitse, was a blessing in disguise. My aunt, my step brother and I were recalled back to Potchefstroom and went to live at a plot called Mooibank, a few kilometres out of town. Two favourable developments occurred. I met my older brother for the first time and I was able to continue with my primary education. It again meant a daily walk and back to the township school this time. The distance to school was a lot shorter than at the farm school. The other pleasure was that on the way I did not have to be taunted by white school children as was the case on the way to Smaldeel. Somehow these children, travelling by bus to a white school further down the road to Kroonstad, derived some fun in insulting these barefooted black children footing to their school. In the winter months, the barefooted learners had learned to warm their feet. As we trudged along, worried that being late would earn you ten lashes with a ruler on the fingers, we would stop when the feet were numb with cold. Our innovative manner to warm the feet and return the normal feeling, was to dig holes in the soft ground with our fingers, then urinate into the hole each one into his own. You would then dip the toes into the warm urine, and relish the return of life to the toes and run faster thereafter. I later appreciated as a doctor that the most peripheral toes or fingers suffer more than other parts of the body when the circulation is compromised.

Life at Von Abo's Farm

The Mpitse house, like all others in the village, was built of mud. The roof was secured with stone rocks on the corrugated iron. Another small outbuilding, a rondavel, serving as a kitchen, was thatch roofed. The walls of all structures were plastered with soft mud. The main house walls would be decorated with patterns inside and outside, all done by hand and occasionally renewed. Cow dung was used to plaster the floors. There were no rooms in the main house. A curtain made of either a blanket or some cloth, separated the adults from the children's sleeping place at night. Sleeping for everybody was on the hard floor, whilst the adults used a mattress. Little boys and little girls slept together. My aunt and uncle slept in another smaller outbuilding. There were no beds for them as well. The children slept naked. School clothes were made by aunt, who would cut the cloth to make a shirt and shorts for boys, and a skirt for a girl. After school, you had to take off your clothes; pack away nicely in some corner, then wrap around a "stert riem" or tshega. This was a long cloth broad in front to cover the private parts, then strung through the natal cleft and tied to a cloth belt. The whole body including the bums, was uncovered. If you felt cold or during all the time in winter time, you would wear a blanket. The little girls wore a thetana. This consisted of strips of" beads", usually dry mealie or bean seeds, threaded through pieces of string, which in turn were tied to a longer string to tie around the waist. The short curtain like strips was to cover the front part only. They too, were naked otherwise. Children past adolescence were privileged to wear simple clothes, especially the girls, whereas, older boys would wear alternately clothes or stert riem. Herding milk cattle and sheep was the boy's chore. The girl's duty was caring for the house. When a cow had calved, there would be milk for porridge, though sour milk was the commoner form, as there were no fridges. Children were fed communally. Aunt or granny would mix everything in one big dish, making sure all the ingredients are well mixed. We tucked into the food, using our hands. A slow eater would starve! Cooking and warming sources was mostly dried cow dung (disu). On this farm, there not enough trees for fire wood. After processing of dried mealies, the bare broken cob centres, were acceptable for making fire. Fire was made in the "lapa" (circle in front, connecting the house units) or in the rondavel. On weekends, we would visit other relatives on the neighbouring farms. Sundays were church days, and on these days or when the pastor from town came (once in three months), means would be made to find a fowl to slaughter. These were occasions to look forward to, as there would be the insides or legs or the head to eat. There certainly would be gravy for the porridge. With some luck, cakes or delicious home baked bread (baked in an ant heap oven) would be available to feast on. The best was always for the visitors first

Further Schooling and Life at Mooibank

The farm, I came to, to live with my grand father, belonged to a Basjan Koster. We lived here with my grand parents. The house was built of mud and stone, also a flat corrugated iron roof. My aunt, Mrs Mpitse passed on to live at her younger sister's place as the second wife of the sister's husband (agreed to by tradition). My brother and I were the only children at my grandparents', and my grand father called me his last borne child. My mother was still lost to a domestic life and her two younger brothers lived elsewhere. We slept in an outbuilding. The farm produced tomatoes and grapes. We enjoyed porridge with gravy made of tomatoes and onions on a regular basis. The general style in the home was like at Von Abo's. There was now, however, a coal stove or a paraffin primus stove. The latter would be used for warming up. Radiation of heat was encouraged by placing a piece of zinc on the stove flame. Warm water for washing was more frequently available. One would bath from head to toes using a cloth and water in a basin. My grand father was wise, full of family history and talkative. I learnt a lot from him about life in general and about the history of the Mokhobos. He was now with his third wife, whom we only knew as Mme Ngojane.

They had no children. His second wife, whose eldest child was my mother, had since died. She had seven children, four girls and three boys. One, Sello, had died and six were left, two males, and four women. My young grand mother subsequently disappeared mysteriously. Her whereabouts remained an unsolved mystery to this day. Even her family, in Bothaville, never knew what happened to her. We were left as three males to fulfil all roles to run the house, work on the farm and me to go to school. Grandpa and I took a two weeks break in 1948 to tour the Free State seeing families and learning about the very complex clan history. Our tour ended in Johannesburg to meet more families and that is when I saw my mother for the first time. I was sixteen years old then. Our relationship with my mother only matured five years later during my medical student years at Wits University.

Some Cultural Practices

The Mpitses had a family routine. Every year, at winter time, the whole family underwent for each person a ritual to protect against witch craft. This entailed induced vomiting and body incisions at "strategic" body parts. Some itchy medicine powder would be rubbed into the wounds. The house was also fortified by the traditional medicine man (always a male). After my uncle's death by lightning stroke, there was of course a special detailed ritual, including the slaughtering of a sheep. There would be a preliminary divining process through the throwing of dry animal bones, after the head of the family had blown into the bag containing these. This ritual was often called into play for special occasions such as weddings. The divination was to see if some jealous person would want to cause harm or just spoil the family fun. The diviner would also explain the cause of any perceived or real unfortunate state of a bad run of ill-luck, or an unexplained illness. The cause or causes of such would be some angry ancestors who would need to be appeased by slaughtering and or performing some ritualistic procedure on the advice of the medicine man. Some time after my uncle's burial,

I had a strange "black out" on my way home. There after I used to get palpitations, especially when it was overcast or about to rain. The diagnosis by the family medicine man (ngaka), was that Molelekoa's "cloud" (lightning stroke machination) had missed me. The intention was to wipe out Phanuel's family, starting with me. I was treated and cured, but the episode strengthened my maternal grandfather's demand that I come back home. The traditional practitioner who rid me of the "cloud's smoke "predicted that I was destined for great a future as I am blessed with a phenomenal brain("rotten brain" in his language). My maternal grandfather, like me, carried a very historic family name. He was Setlaelo Daniel Mokhobo, the brother of Kubedi, the first borne child of Pampiri Mokhobo. At Setlaelo's household, there were no traditional practices, as he was a devout Christian. The only routine health practice was to give us castor oil at designated intervals to cleanse the inside. I was, however, later to be under the care of my mother's younger sister's husband. This was Mr Shadrack Sesmane Moleko, who took the widow of Phanuel as his spouse (a practice called "sea ntlo", that is entering a house). He was a renowned diviner and traditional practitioner. He also predicted that I would prosper educationally and even one day "ride a large bird" (presumably fly by aeroplane), as a rare feat. He sired three children with my aunt, Mrs Mpitse, a son and two daughters. My maternal uncles (malomes), Setlaelo's sons, also practiced both Christianity and traditional beliefs like the elderly Mpitses. They were two and younger than my mother. They lived on their own away from home, and seldom visited. Grandfather, who was a polygamist, had seven children by his second wife (my mother's mother). He had had a first wife who bore him one son, Letsoko. This chap was generally aloof, kept away from us all. He lived at a farm outside Potchefstroom, to the east. It was called, Haartebeesfontein, and was owned by the Grimbeeck brothers.

Primary and High School Education

Boy Mokhobo at high school, Potchefstroom, 1950

Back home at Mooibank, I enrolled at the then Bantu Primary School in the township. I condensed the school years through a system of promotions and wrote the standard six examinations, an external examination in those days, obtaining a historic first class pass. This made history for the school in 1946. My success was made possible by Mr Shadrack Moleko's regular administration of protective medicines against all possible evils, likely to emanate from jealous individuals. Standard six was to be the end of my career. Grandfather found work for me at Haartebeesfontein, where I worked for a Mr Ntsoelengoe, a foreman on another plot next to the Grimbeecks. My job was to lead a span of oxen to plough, a highly exacting and dangerous role. If you stumbled, the oxen would trample you to death. But, I survived. Shortly before my standard six examinations, some stroke of luck had been thrown my way in some mysterious way. A Mr Simon McDover Lekhela, recruited out of Fort Hare, had started with a few students for Junior

Certificate at the Bantu Secondary School. This Bantu Secondary School started at about the time I was in Standard four. It was struggling as the pass rate for standard six was poor, so those who enrolled for Junior Certificate were randomly chosen. I was six months into my farm working life when an uncle, my mother's brother, Pampiri came to inform Mr Ntsoelengoe that Mr Lekhela has sent him to fetch me. Indeed, I came to join the class, Form one after the June holidays. My uncle gave me his old clothes. The trousers I could alter to my desired designs (length and leg width). The jackets I had to wear as "jas baitjies" (coat-cum-jacket) with folded sleeves. Long pants, jas baitjies, no shoes, were Patrick's typical appearance. The trouser alterations were sown with a certain Mrs Sepotokele's "trap" machine. Her son, William Potoki Sepotokele had become my friend and we did the tailoring together. School fees, books and necessary goodies were an obvious problem. However, I soon learned to fend for myself as a golf caddie and three times a week worked as a "garden boy". With my stint as a farm labourer, I had also earned six bags of mealies. These provided enough food for quite some time. I worked as a garden boy for a Mnr Kuhn, earning ten shillings a month and had one good meal on the day. The caddying money was a pitiful one shilling and six pence for eighteen holes, but nevertheless added a welcome amount to meet my needs. I therefore settled into my school work without money worries, made Form one in half a year, and proceeded to pass the Junior Certificate with first class in 1949. I had not disappointed Mr Lekhela. In fact, the class of 1949 made him proud, producing nine clear passes (the biggest number ever) plus a first class for the first time, by one Patrick Mokhobo. The latter was working afternoons as a garden boy, and as a golf caddy at the local golf course twice weekly. By now, Mr Kubedi Patrick Mokhobo had matured and become prosperous in many ways. He looked after his money, and used it wisely. He afforded fitting clothes and bought a pair of white and brown sharp pointed shoes. The sharp points though smart, were a bad choice for the feet that had never "felt" a shoe for fifteen years. The toes had spread widely, so the gentleman earned

himself permanent corns! When half way through Form two, my other
uncle, Ezekiel, the youngest in my mother's line got married, secured a
room for renting at the house of one Mr Frank Mogoje. So, I came to
live with them in the township. Mr Lekhela was a disciplinarian and a
teaching School principal. He was also a perfectionist who wanted and
demanded high standards. He taught English and history with a passion
and a distinctive style.

Township Life, Secondary School

Uncle Ezekiel Mokhobo rented a room large enough to serve as a
large bedroom for the couple and three children, myself and two girls
from his wife's side. On many occasions, there would be other relatives'
children visiting from the farms, often swelling the inmates' numbers
to seven bodies! The style again was to provide for a curtain blanket
or cloth enclosure for the adults at night and spread the children by
gender groups on the floor. This time there was a bed for adults, hoisted
on bricks to provide storage for our bedding under it during the day.
There was an eating table, four chairs and a coal stove in the corner.
At one corner was a makeshift wardrobe. The corner was turned into
some triangular form with a cloth hung from the wall. The clothes were
hung here, or folded and placed on the floor. At sleeping time the table
was pushed into a corner and the chairs placed on top. There was no
electricity. As the oldest child, a secondary school learner, I had to find
a way to study at night. Fortunately, my uncle had late nights as a hotel
waiter. So, it was not a major disturbance or inconvenience to others,
if I sat by the table, by dim candle light and study until uncle arrived.
Sometimes, I would "force" to study next to the stove whilst aunt
(uncle's wife) is cooking! I have a burn scar on the thigh as a relic of oil
splashing off the pan when aunt was frying fat cakes (magwenya)!This
was the life for eighteen months up to the historic pass. This was
when Mr Lekhela's efforts were rewarded. Nine out of twelve Junior
Certificate (JC) students passed, including Patrick Mokhobo who

notched a first class pass with two distinctions. Another stroke of luck occurred, unbelievable as it may sound. Mr Lekhela, encouraged by the 1949 class achievement took a brave decision to experiment with us for Matriculation. Five of us enrolled. He offered me a bursary also, as the school fees of two pounds a year were high and there were the books to buy. My earnings would not be enough, as I had also decided to provide space at my uncle's room, by renting a room at Mrs Sepotokeles. This also meant taking a number of things on credit, a bed, and the where withal, plus pots, cutlery, a primus stove and several necessities, had to be bought. I also had to budget for food, paraffin, toiletry, candles, as well as renovating the place. Being independent and self sufficient, was now a firmly rooted characteristic in my makeup.

Bantu Secondary School and the Experiment

University, 1954

The Form IV class of five students was taught by the teachers of the Junior Certificate stream. These scanty staffs were stretched to the limits.

It was rumoured that black students who wrote the Senior Certificate of the Transvaal Education Department (TED) at various black high schools in the province failed in large numbers and that of those who passed; very few managed an exemption pass. Here comes my lucky break again! Despite difficulties raised by the TED, which controlled education at the time, Mr Lekhela registered us for the newly discovered "black friendly" Joint Matriculation Board (JMB) examination. With the belief that TED white examiners victimised students from black schools unfairly, many of these had gradually opted for the JMB. The results were reportedly better, at least as regards the numbers passing and the percentage obtaining an exemption pass. The Bantu Secondary School teachers had to double up in 1950 for two groups, namely, three for J C (three classes) plus Form iv. The number increased to four groups in 1951. Several of these teachers did not have degrees. Our subjects included zoology and botany. There was no library, and there were no laboratories. Much innovation was needed for learning. We went to the veldt to catch whatever suitable animal for zoology, be it a frog, a lizard or we picked up a dead dog or cat. For botany the nearby veldt was full of flowers. Afternoon preparations were compulsory, thus Mr Lekhela earned a nickname, "Prep". He was also known as "Skot". At about this time, the school was electrified. What luck was this! Patrick Mokhobo is made the class prefect and is entrusted with the keys to the study hall. I was to lock up after studies and open early next morning. A golden opportunity presented itself! I could forgo the candles and study all by myself, in the quiet night at the school class room. God was always on my side. I was blessed that so many unintended unforeseen events continued to shape my life. Indeed, coming from nowhere, I seemed to be destined to go somewhere. We wrote our examinations eventually and three of the five passed, one exemption, one school leaving pass and one clear pass, aggregate symbol B and a distinction in zoology! It emerged afterwards that, although in that year 1951, there were first class passes at several black schools, there were no distinctions. Also, this Bantu Secondary School class of 1951 was the first and remained as the last for a number of years to come. This one distinction story served to exaggerate the achievement of the student from Potchefstroom. The newspapers made undue sensationalised noise.

A boy at high school 1950, Mokhobo first year
University of the Witwatersrand 1953

The local paper, the Potchefstroom herald picked up the story, "buttered" with the fact that the achiever was an orphan who had studied by candle light. The true part of the story was about my having shown initiative in fending for me. I thank Mr Lekhela for spreading the news in this manner, as the sensation was another lucky stroke for me as a local businessman and garage owner, who happened to be Jewish, Mr Hugh Calderbank got interested in this ambitious youngster who had put the town on the map. He heard that the boy had aspirations of being a doctor. Fortunately it was not revealed that Patrick had been rescued from being sent to a reformatory. In 1950 Patrick and other naughty boys, had stolen fish from a cafe close to the school. The magistrate on receiving a report by a young white female social worker, sentenced

Patrick to be rehabilitated by the school principal! The social worker's report was based on the dire findings related to the overcrowded family single room of my uncle's. Another minor offence was when I was arrested on my way from the Grimbeecks for failing to produce a pass (native ID). This happened on a Friday, which meant spending three nights in prison, and was released on Monday after testimony by Mr Lekhela that I am a school boy. The dark side of my life at this stage was these two occasions when I experienced prison conditions. I had not applied to any university, as I only had the dream, but knew I would have no means. A last minute approach at the University of the Witwatersrand (Wits) was unsuccessful. It was January and applications had closed the previous year. We had driven with Mr Calderbank in his car together with Mr Lekhela. I remember Mr Calderbank stopping at Uncle Charlies' restaurant. We would not be served of course. So he brought the food to the car. At the Witwatersrand (Wits) medical school, we were received by a sympathetic Professor Teddy (Theodore) Gilman, who advised that I try Fort Hare, get minimum credits in the four basic sciences and try Wits the following year, as there was a standing arrangement in this regard. For those who could not meet the required minimum credits, a complete BSc, finished in regulation time would enable the candidate to be considered for admission into the second year of study. I was accepted at Fort Hare, called at the time, the South African Native College (SANC), affiliated to Rhodes University. I was pleasantly surprised to be admitted having applied that late. But, in retrospect, I regard this as part of the chain of fortunate events.

FORT HARE, OR SANC

Preparations for the journey started. Mr Calderbank took me to a men's shop, Hepworth's. I was clothed from head to feet. I got a wide brimmed hat, a black and stripe double breasted suit, shoes and socks. Strange clothes, seen for the first time, included vests, underpants, and something called "pyjamas". On the Fort Hare list, the latter taxed my mind as to what this was. I did recognise the bedding requirements. The journey to Alice was by train, having boarded the steam engine train from Potchefstroom to Park Station, Johannesburg. The trip was not remarkable as one's thought were dominated by anticipatory excitement. Student life at SANC for the year I spent there was brief but a very enriching experience. Students came from all the provinces, southern African states and even Africa to the north of the Limpopo River and East Africa. It was the year of the defiance campaign, 1952. There were a few South African "coloured" citizens with a dominant black student body. I stayed at a Methodist church hostel. There was some cultural division between the students from the Johannesburg townships and "other" less informed "skappies" from smaller towns or rural areas. The ANC Youth League was dominant. Fortunately I had been introduced to struggle politics from home already. The first "non-white" doctor to qualify and practice in Potchefstroom, Dr A H Bismilla, a graduate of Wits, arrived in 1949. He recruited a few of us into the youth wing of the Unity Movement (Non-European Unity Movement), called Society of Young Africa (SOYA). This body espoused south African non-racialism, had a highly philosophic economic approach to Apartheid, believing that economics and not race was the basis for oppression. In my final matriculation year, however, four church members from Evaton, Wilberforce Institution, came to the township, at the mission house, where a meeting took place after the service. From their presentation as ANC Youth Leaguers, a number of us found theirs a more appealing political philosophy, giving more emphasis and recognition to oppression of the black majority. I was at home in the Fort Hare student culture including the ruling politics, although by nature I am not an activist, preferring a pragmatic open-minded accommodating style rather. There were a few SOYANS, but were dominated completely. I decided to give my commitment at SANC my hundred percent focus. Unlike my classmates from better schools, I had not done Physical Science. Apparently at other schools, those intending to study medicine joined a stream that offered biology and physical science. I found Physics 1 particularly steep. The lecturer, a Professor Davidson did not make things easy for anybody. He rushed, mumbled to himself, completed the solutions and left. Our relationship with the lecturers was generally cold. As it turned out, although I managed the required credits in all the four subjects, my lowest mark was in physics. The student life at Fort Hare was pleasant and complete with a sense of total belonging. The majority lecturers were white, with one in mathematics and another junior lecturer in physics being the only blacks in the science faculty.

ENTRY TO WITS

I came back home in December, not knowing what would happen next regarding my ambition. There was certainly no money, unless my benefactor would be willing to pay the more expensive tuition fees at Wits for at least five years. To add to my anxiety, somehow my results from SANC either got lost or I was facing an unlucky situation for the first time. After Fort Hare, I also had some sense of guilt about accepting free financial help from a white man. This was the influence of the country politics of the Defiance Campaign and the seeming core philosophy of the ANC Youth League as I understood it. In many respects oppression was colour based. So I set tight, did not wish to contact Mr Calderbank yet, especially before I got my official results. Also, when I left for Fort Hare he had asked me not to "get into politics". Fort Hare was known for its quasi-anti-white politics even in a small town like Potchefstroom. Of course my benefactor was not aware that I was already initiated into politics from home, albeit in a somewhat diluted manner. The SOYA philosophy was gentle on apartheid and as a new recruit to the Youth League, I took their philosophy in a "raw" manner.

Through Mr Lekhela's help we got to obtain my results and submitted these to Wits. I also got to know about a possible scholarship offered by the Mendi Memorial Fund, and duly applied, but got no response. However, my hope was somehow kindled. My opportunities had also been sponsored by the news in the

Johannesburg based papers. For example the Star newspaper ran
an article about the wonder boy from a disadvantaged background.
It went on to print a caption "brilliant medical career foreshadowed
for a Native", although the facts were a bit mixed up with another
fellow who was going to Natal Medical School the same year, Pascal
Ngakane, where Professor Gillman was the first Dean. My stroke
of luck being admitted to Wits despite a late submission of my first
year results, were captured in the star newspaper edition of 13th
February 1953, "Lucky error for Native student". It reported that my
initial results were incorrect, not reflecting that I had obtained the
required credits and my initial disappointment had been dissipated
also by the award of a scholarship. Indeed my chain of lucky breaks
had resurfaced! Wits accepted me and in addition offered me a loan
scholarship. The year 1952 was a turning point for black medical
study aspirants. The largest number of blacks were admitted into
first year into Wits. It so happened that the white students (majority
Jewish) had set up a financing mechanism by establishing a fund, the
African Medical Students Trust Fund (AMSTF), specifically to help
black medical students. The loan awarded would be interest free. Like
Esther in the old Testament, who saved the Jews from extermination,
for my personal salvation, I was at the right time at the right place
to have my ambitions salvaged by a gesture of Jewish students. I was
awarded a scholarship. An additional factor for my fortunate break
was the fate that befell my fellow Africans. The African first year
students at Wits, almost all failed to qualify for entry into second
year. So, there I was, receiving a golden opening together with five
other black students from Fort Hare who had completed a BSc degree
in regulation time. I guess, due to the high failures, there were not
many takers eligible that year from within Wits. We were six blacks
admitted in 1953. This number was constant throughout, with six
other "non-whites" (always Indians), making it twelve out of a class
of one hundred. There was no official quota system, we were told.
During my stay at Wits, it was odd that the other six "non-African"

slots would include a "coloured" if available. The Indian students paid for themselves, as would some coloureds, or obtain their own financing by way of bank loans. The number twelve was constant, even including those who failed and repeated. The Johannesburg City Council also offered two scholarships on an adhoc basis to bonafide residents of the townships.

THE WITS DAYS

I did re-connect with Mr Calderbank, and would see him at his garage business when on vacation. Ours was like a business relationship. I never got to know where he lived and never met his family. He was happy for me that I had found a sponsor. I was comfortable with the situation where I had borrowed money from an "anonymous" white "person. The Potchefstroom environment, with its harsh racial divide, also encouraged the aloofness between me and my first sponsor. Some places in Potchefstroom prominently barred Africans. This included any eating place and a number of shops. The few shops that tolerated taking your money as a black, allowed you to buy through the window. Buying clothes was a problem, as you were not allowed to fit. I was fortunate that I could "point" at my clothes for Fort Hare, and they did fit. Student life at Wits was drastically different from the life at SANC. Blacks were seen and not heard, so to speak. The white students spoke about us and on our behalf. Student Representative Councillors were white throughout (SRC). In fact, the non-white issues dominated the elections, and divided liberal thinking from conservative attitudes. This situation was bolstered by the fact that "conservative" faculties, such as engineering, had for a long time not admitted a single non-white. There was an occasional black face in some faculty like law or education, or African studies. The liberal political slogan emphasized "academic non-segregation", which by implication accepted social segregation. One developed the attitude that as a black or non-white, your purpose at

Wits was to come get your degree and go to your own kind elsewhere. The city of Johannesburg was a far cry from the harsh racism of Potchefstroom. The user-friendly atmosphere for blacks was consolidated by the surrounding non-white areas such as Fordsburg, Ferreirastown, Mayfair and others, where you could dine or have a drink (not alcohol) or attend cinema. These areas had a large Indian resident community with businesses. At Fordsburg or "Fietus" were a few Chinese trading areas. There was also, Mayfair, with predominantly Indian residents.

There was a non-white residence for Wits students, Douglas Smit House, occupied mainly by blacks (never an Indian student). Blacks were mainly south Africans, and an occasional foreign student on a government sponsorship. The black students of the University held their own social functions at the Great Hall. Black and white socialising was at absolute minimum outside the University. Occassionally, a white student would also be risking arrest by entertaining a black fellow student at his/her house. The black student would also be running the risk of being arrested for loitering (night special pass) at night on the way back. So-called white liquor was taboo of course, in "any container".

Conformity with the law of the government, was reflected in the annual Rag. There was a non-white float, happily "accepted" as normal.

The first year involved dissection. The cadavers were all black bodies. In the pathology year, there were autopsy procedures. If the corpse was a white body, non-whites would not be allowed to witness. They would be called in to see the internal organs only after the body had been removed. An occasional "near disaster" would occur, when proper prior home work was not done. The lecturer would peep under the white sheet, and lo and behold the body is of a white person! The non-whites would "politely" be asked to leave. We co-operated without a murmur of protest, literally walk out tails between our legs, and "happily" return to learn whatever there was to know from the internal organs only, as these were anonymous enough. In the clinical years, the separation continued. Non-whites went to black hospitals to see black patients only. The white students had the privilege of double exposure, by examining both white and black patients. This blatantly unequal teaching was normal business as usual. Besides, the non-whites seldom met Clinical Heads of departments, as these were based at the white hospitals. This was a deficiency and a disadvantage nobody seemed to worry about from both sides. The non-white students were tolerated and they tolerated the situation, because theirs was to get the degree under any circumstances and pass on to their own kind in practice, in their own environment. So, the five years at Wits were tolerably "smooth". A lot of the friendships formed across the colour line and lasted for many years after medical school.

Graduation first medical degree 1957 Mokhobo with benefactor Mr Hugh Cakderbank (deceased)

Mokhobo, first wife, and benefactor at same graduation ceremony

The graduation ceremony was a usual multi-racial affair in the University Great Hall. My benefactor was my other guest with my wife. We were allowed only two guests each. The newspapers recounted the story of 1952. The Golden City Post had an article headed "Dr Patrick Repays A White Man's Faith!" It repeated the story as to how I made matriculation under difficult social conditions. The story was laced with the facts of my early life, the role of Mr Lekhela, and the help provided by a middle aged European who was quoted to have said "I regard the young man as my son", and further saying "I was impressed by this little boy's meteoric progress through school" and that "Patrick has repaid me a million times with his achievement". The Golden City Post newspaper mentioned other nine non-white graduands, one of whom, Dr Allen Nxumalo was to become the Minister of Health in independent Swaziland, his country of origin and my saviour. There was a lovely picture taken of "the new doctor", his wife and benefactor in the City Post edition of the 15th December 1957.

THE CITY OF JOHANNESBURG

The city and its surrounding townships were always a happy distraction, where one felt at home. I had many relatives to visit, travelling by bus or train to Sophiatown, Western Native Township or far west Soweto. I saw my mother very frequently in the northern suburbs. Interestingly, she worked for Jewish employers throughout the thirty two years she was a domestic servant. She slept in a room on the premises, on a bed hoisted on bricks to create storage space under the bed. I got to know the employer she worked for longest, the Skok family. They were amused that my mother had a son studying to be a doctor at a white University. Nevertheless, when I visited, I used the tradesman's entrance and never entered the house. There were "double decker" buses, in which if multi-racial, the blacks would sit on the deck. My mother did general work for the Skoks, including cooking. However, she was bought special cheap meat cuts to cook for herself separately. This was slightly different from the dog's meat. We however, regarded all of this servant's food as dog food. There would be an occasion when my mother and I savoured the remains of the food she had prepared for the employers. She, like me at home, used a primus stove to cook her food and for warming the room. Her clothes hung in a makeshift wardrobe in a corner. In many respects the environments in the "rich" northern suburbs were no different from the one obtaining at Potchefstroom location for us, except for the cleaner air to breathe.

THE CHURCH IN THE CONTEXT SO FAR

I was baptised at the age of nine months. Church attendance on Sundays was compulsory on the farms. In my later years at the Potchefstroom location, attendance was voluntary and enjoyable. I attended Sunday school, sang in the choir and attended Sunday services of the A M E Church which were held three times on Sundays. On some Sunday afternoons, an important soccer match would take preference. At Fort Hare, in the hostel there were evening prayers. At the primary school and secondary school, there were morning prayers at assembly. After re-connecting with my mother, church attendance with her on Sundays was a voluntary routine. The services were either in down town Johannesburg or in Sophiatown, which was the nearest township. This churchianity became a permanent component of my life forever. In my fourth year of study, as was the practice by many black students, I left Douglas Smit Hostel, to rent a room in Sophiatown and became a full member of that congregation. The scholarship provided pocket money which was enough to meet personal needs and books. The scholarship also paid the hostel fees. So when one stayed on your own, the allowance plus the hostel fees into your hands, was quite generous. Hence, even clothes, one could afford without having to caddy or do other holiday jobs at home. The room I rented in Sophiatown, 41 Morris Street, there being just one of the few still remaining during the removals. The other rooms of the house were rented by journalists, including the famous journalist, Can Themba and others. The experience was of its own kind, but the church was my bulwark. I missed the tragic event as a result, where a medical student, Mr J J T Jabavu was stabbed to death by a famous "tsotsi" (Mthembu) at a shebeen house. There was a feeling or notion that as a medical student, you had to mix with these gangsters for "protection". Hence a number of medical students, like Mr Jabavu, got involved in bad company.

THE FROM NOWHERE TO SOMEWHERE IN PERSPECTIVE, LUCKY BREAKS

The relocation to the Transvaal in 1944 was as a result of my stepfather's death and the decision by my grandfather to reclaim me. Therefore continuing with education beyond standard two, was pure luck. The practice at Von Abo's farm was to provide only four years of schooling for workers children, then be indentured at any age as farm worker, through a process called "ankort". An uncle got some divine visitation to come and rescue me from another possibly permanent farm working life in 1947, after a stint with Mr Ntsoelengoe as a farm hand. Mr Lekhela's experiment of 1950 was a divine gift, because the next step after JC would have been finding work in town, hopefully appropriate for the level of literacy. The exaggerated publicity about my matriculation results did the penultimate trick and made the wonderful gesture of Mr Calderbank possible, himself a lone human star in a town steeped in racial intolerance and prejudices. The disastrous results of the black first year students at Wits just paved the "wonder boy's" route of destiny! I shudder to think that I would have had to find funds to complete the Bsc degree at Fort Hare, from somewhere. Perhaps Mr Calderbank would have agreed to continue. I can't guess. Besides, I had by this time committed an ideological sin in my mind, as a result of the politics of the time, being young and immature. From my side it would have been difficult to continue to accept Mr Calderbank's direct help.

THE ROAD OPENS FOR THE NEW DOCTOR

Mokhobo and the three kids of the first marriage, picture
taken in the township before going back to specialise and
qualified as a Specialist Physician-Cardiologist

The medical degree is obtained plus a prize, the William Craib
prize for the best African student of the year in medicine, 1957. The
previous two years had been another favourable development in good
time. All non-european graduates had to go to some mission hospital
for internship. These were found in Natal and Eastern Cape quite an

inconvenience for many. Besides, I was now married and had six months old boy, and my wife was still to complete her social work degree.

Drs N H Motlana and D Mji had timeously exploded an anomaly in 1955, whereby Africans were not allowed to do internship at Baragwanath Hospital, or any government hospital in the Transvaal. The reasons were that African doctors would give orders to white nurses, and this would be in conflict with the apartheid's philosophy of white superiority. Luckily, therefore, in 1957, Baragwanath Hospital had opened the doors for black interns. The authorities, however, had given all white nurses accelerated promotions as matrons, thus removing them from the wards. So, they would not have to take orders from black doctors. This lucky break (another of many), allowed me to be near my family, as I undertook my first Baragwanath Hospital stint in 1958.

INTERNSHIP, BARAGWANATH HOSPITAL

This largest hospital in the southern hemisphere, was a rich source of clinical material. However, I always hungered for the experience on white patients' health or illness profiles. There was accommodation provided, with a total separation of races. All senior doctors were white. At tea break and lunch, the doctors went though separate doors to segregated facilities. Such were the physical facilities. There was never a murmur of complaint from anybody, and no comment about the unequal teaching. After all, it was a continuation of the medical school system. We, the black juniors knew that we missed on the more refined discussion of problem cases over a cup of tea or plate of food. There was nothing spectacular about this stint at Baragwanath Hospital.

I was married, earning a so-called marriage allowance. My package was equal to fifty percent of a white colleague's, whilst other non-whites earned the equivalent of two thirds a white colleague's salary. My child was taken to my in-laws in Lady Selborne in Pretoria, and my wife stayed on at Douglas Smit House. We spent weekends together at her parent's place, whenever I was free. We had gotten married the traditional way plus by Christian rites, married by an Anglican priest. I paid my own lobola, to the tune of fifty pounds. The wedding celebrations were held in the new Potchefstroom township of Ikageng. It was a very happy occasion with the usual types of food in abundance plus African beer. My uncles and other relatives had made contributions towards the food. Even the beast was donated by one family member. So the financial burden was not great. My mother was now fully integrated with the son and daughter-in-law, grandson and my wife's family. She was elated when she was asked to retire and move with us to Benoni, where I set up solo private practice in 1959.

GENERAL PRACTICE

Mokhobo's house in a township when a general practitioner, 1959-1961

My next move cannot be described as either a lucky break or not. It was simply being a victim of the pass laws, the Urban Areas Act. I had decided that Soweto would be the place to set up practice. I had had the exposure to the environment when I did locums for Dr Nthato Motlana. Under section 10(d) of the said act, I did not qualify to stay or practice in Soweto. I tolerated numerous degrading visits to the pass office at No. 80 Albert Street. My efforts were fruitless, and frustrating. I was desperate. Perhaps the gods or ancestors were angry with me for not going back to plough back my skills for the benefit of the community at home. It did not cross my mind that I should get guidance from some diviner or traditional practitioner. My uncle, husband to my mother's younger sister would have obliged. Besides, I still trusted him.

For reasons not known to me, I was not interested in going back to my roots, which were now at the new township of Ikageng. The old township with all its historic features, the school, the churches and places dear to my childhood, had been flattened. My grandfather had retired. He went to live with the son by his first wife at the Grimbeecks. My brother, who now worked as a qualified shoe repairer, at the nearby industrial area, was staying with my uncle (malome), the youngest of my grandfathers seven children by his second wife, my mothers mother. The family house in Ikageng was a four roomed match box type structure. This was a definite upgrade from the one room dwelling place at the old location, the latter subsequently named Willemklopperville. It was so named after the Location Superintendent, Mnr Willem Klopper. This was a remarkable Afrikaner. He showed unusual interest in the educational progress of the blacks. To this end he had donated an annual prize for the best all-round scholar of the year at the Bantu Secondary School. I was to be the first proud recipient of this privilege in 1950, as a victor laudorum and was given a springbok watch. This was to be my treasured watch for many years, through all my schooling up to the period I started practice.

I opted for the East Rand, Benoni, a small town. An uncle, Rev. Mokhodi, a pastor of the DRC gave me temporary accommodation at Etwatwa, the oldest location. This was before the inhabitants were removed to Daveyton, a new township. I obtained a match box type municipal house in Daveyton, in the main street, Eiselen Street, as a surgery. I did not encounter influx control hurdles this time. After about three months, I also got another four roomed match box type municipal house in Tebele Street as a dwelling. My retired mother joined me and my wife completed her degree end of 1958. The family unit of four lived together for the first time. Daveyton was a classical Verwoerdian type of township, divided into separate tribal sections in keeping with the apartheid philosophy. The majority of the early inhabitants of Daveyton were a collection of displaced farm labourers. Soon, the numbers increased as Etwatwa people without own property came by own volition, and stand owners were gradually but forcibly moved and some people also came from the other nearby black settlements. I was the second black doctor in the Benoni townships. At the nearby white owned shopping complex, were two white doctors' partnership practices. I also took part time sessions at the newly built local clinic, where there was one fulltime white doctor. The experience as a general practitioner turned out to be challenging. The socio-economic conditions were primitive. There was no running water in the houses, with an outside toilet for each household. There was electric street lighting and basic electrification of housing units. However, unemployment was high, hence rampant poverty and high rate of malnutrition prevailed, especially among unbreastfed babies and young children. After a year's solo practice, Dr Dumisani Mzamane joined me.

We tried to run our practice as rationally and scientifically as was possible. We worked seven days a week. We took alternate weekends off, and alternated night calls. The latter was of no use as prospective patients came on foot to knock at the nearest doctor's door. We attended to all age groups, and all genders. The scope of practice included common ailments, minor operations such as wound suturing, removal of benign growths and circumcisions (medical and social or cosmetic). We delivered babies in the houses, in most cases and very often on the floor, with candle light, where a match box structure had been extended, but the owner had no money to install electricity in the new rooms. We consulted at the rooms and also did house calls. We charged ten shillings for a child's or baby's consultation, at the rooms, inclusive of an injection of whatever and one or two bottles of medicine. For adults at the rooms, we charged fifteen shillings. This covered the consultation fee, a must injection plus pills and a bottle of medicine, often laced with aloes, because the bitter, the more effective the medicine. Repeat visits for injections, usually an antibiotic or a demanded injection (vitamin by our choice) was five shillings. Any home visit was one pound for a daytime call and one pound five shillings for an after hours and weekend call. The fees included a standard dispensing as above. For a delivery the charge was five pounds, which would often be paid by instalments during ante-natal checks. We dispensed skim milk for free to kwashiorkor cases. A circumcision was five pounds, wound suturing one pound ten shillings. We gave credit regularly if requested, though the payment rate was low. The debt was often only remembered next, when there was an illness in the family, which could be after many months. Even then, the old credit in part or whole would be offered and the new consultation be asked to be put on credit. Sometimes payment in kind was offered. The item could be something decorative (flower pot, a traditional work of art). We were compelled some times to collect some household item as security for the debt. We soon abandoned this practice, when our surgery got full of chairs, clothing items, some kitchen ware or whatever we deemed likely to ensure early "release "by paying the debt.

We befriended local traditional medicine men and women and worked together on common problems. These were for functional, emotional, or stress related disorders, or even mental illnesses. We co-operated with the beliefs of our patients, in a manner that would not compromise treatment for organic disease, because we ended providing medical certificates. We would also diplomatically discourage wrong methods of treatment, such as giving enemas to babies suffering from diarrhoea. We would connive with muti grease on the baby's fontanelle or skin incisions on safe areas with local hygiene ensured.

We ourselves would resort to some innovative unconventional form of treatment when we are stuck. For example, a traditional midwife delivered woman, then, severe postpartum bleeding, followed. The doctor would have clean underpants or doek plugged into the vagina before the patient being shipped off to hospital. The ambulance services were poor, with always interminable delays. We put up scalp drips on dehydrated babies at the rooms and have the mothers nurse them overnight. Sick pneumonias were put on drips for intravenous antibiotics at home, the bottle being hung on a nail knocked into the wall. This unfortunately involved two or three visits per day, with or without payment. We did charge extra for these "expensive" extra forms of treatment, if possible, but our concern was to save lives regardless. Sometimes we preferred to carry a sick patient to the rooms in our car. We prepared our own oral rehydration fluid with salt and sugar water. Sometimes we preferred to give such by intra-gastric tube, or via the peritoneum.

The referral hospital was the Boksburg-Benoni Hospital some twenty miles away. The staff (both doctors and nurses) was very short and treatment was not always to our satisfaction. We had a notion that this facility, which was run by an all white medical doctor team, was hostile to us.

Our neighbour white general practitioners were allowed sessions there. On many instances events strengthened our suspicions. Either it was just the system or people, but many episodes of apparent neglect occurred.

For example, a patient we referred with a dislocated mandible from extreme yawning, was found still sitted open mouthed at casualty after twenty four hours! The perceived atmosphere definitely improved after the arrival of Dr Ivor Kaplan, a Wits graduate. He was reachable, communicated with us on medical referrals, which formed the bulk of our patients. We thus stopped trying to treat serious cases in the patients' homes, saving ourselves stress, time and unpaid bills. We had to write off many debts, though.

ASPECTS OF LIFE IN DAVEYTON

There were very few African doctors. In Daveyton, we were three, there being a Dr Mafu Dotwana in solo practice, the first to open practice here. He was the first to set up practice. Of course my practice would not have prospered had I neglected calling in my muti man, Mr Sesman Moleko to do as tradition required. He came all the way from a farm outside Potchefstroom and doctored the rooms. This was just before Dr Mzamane joined me. Indeed my practice picked up overnight to such a level that I decided to discontinue sessions at the local clinic. The arrival of Dr Mzamane also boosted the practice. There was always a belief that a "new" doctor comes with better skills. In addition, those who owed one doctor, would prefer to consult the new one, who would possibly trust them with another credit! A number of patients would end up owing many doctors. When the list of doctors is exhausted, the "oldest" would be tried, in case he does not remember the previous consultation! Such shopping around was common.

A new challenge or challenges emerged. There was community pressure to provide badly needed leadership. The doctor, as an enlightened person, independent in many ways, especially not a government employee, was an obvious choice. This was the same doctor who was consulted for his wisdom on several non-medical social issues. People consulted on domestic matters, marital problems and sought advice about further schooling for their children, or even how best to invest their moneys. Indeed the doctor was regarded as the

47

natural leader, a trusted expert, a social worker, marriage counsellor, a constant ray of hope for the future, and a political leader. I yielded to this pressure, accepting the evil that whilst apartheid could not yet be defeated, one could "join" them with a clear conscience. I thus became chairman of a school committee, a member of the school board and a member of the advisory board. I contained this "collaboration", even as a founder member of the Pan Africanist Congress (PAC) of 1959. I was also in the central committee of the movement and headed a portfolio for fundraising with Drs Peter Tsele, Lancelot Gama and one Mr Monde Jolobe. We opened Daveyton a cell. Some of my patients were in the special branch (SB) of the secret police. They informed me that my treacherous political activities were being watched. They obliged with "advice" that I not use my car when going to meetings, rather thumb a lift, so that I do not have to be "quarantined" (watched closely). This may have helped, as hard evidence to nab me was hard to come by (people's good doctor) or my special branch patients connived. In fact, the chief SB, one Col. Koloane was a regular patient, as was Sgt Bohloko, assistant station commander. Thus in the swoop of 1960, I was miraculously left out. In course of time my ambition to specialise got stronger and I had many other reasons to be restless. There was also the socio-political conflict. An unexpected social scandal also befell me as well.

My wife suspected that one clinic nurse; Ms Matilda Monaheng was my secret lover. She schemed with her friend to apply drastic measures as a solution. The poor nurse was lured to my house and had her face burned with hot porridge, and was permanently scarred. I had to meet the subsequent costs at plastic surgery attempt. Besides, my wife was locked up, and I paid bail. Through a lawyer friend, Mr Godfrey Pitje, we got an expensive but best criminal lawyer and a comrade, Adv. Joe Slovo to defend. In addition, I got my traditional medicine man, Mr Moleko to come do the necessary ritual. Mrs Mokhobo was acquitted! I had no choice but headed for Baragwanath Hospital in 1962, much to the disappointment of the community at large. A Dr Kgosi Dalamba joined Dr Mzamane. There was no "good will" or sale money to paid Dalamba subsequently immigrated to Canada and was succeeded by Dr Phineas Nene.

THE SECOND BARAGWANATH STINT, 1962-1967

I was called for an interview at Baragwanath hospital. The panel was a high powered group consisting of clinical heads, and TPA (Transvaal Provincial Administration) officials. I was questioned about my intention to specialise in a manner that suggested I was a strange phenomenon, or a freak or some novelty. There had been no experience about Africans wanting to specialise. However, despite my age and experience, I was offered a Senior Medical Officer's post in paediatrics, which I indicated as my first choice. If I was white I would have walked into a registrar's post right away. The requirements for such a post were two years experience after internship. It should have been automatic to walk into this post being qualified for five years. I accepted the experiment with resigned willingness. Unfortunately the two heads of this department made me feel unwanted. I must say that I was not surprised, as the signals were evident at the interview. After six months, I switched to Internal Medicine, where the head, a conservative Englishman, Dr V H Wilson was keen to sponsor this ambitious black man. After another six months, Dr Wilson accorded me a registrar's post. I thus worked for a year as SHO, during which time I had a difficult time working under junior, young, inexperienced white registrars, who did not impress me with their knowledge either. I learnt to be courteous and diplomatic lest I spoil my rare chances. I knuckled down to the business of equipping myself, ignoring all else, took everything in my stride and focussed on the primary purpose for which I had come. The residences were still separate. We dined separately and had separate tea rooms. There were now a sprinkling of black interns, mainly Africans who had qualified from the Natal Medical School. This facility had opened in 1950.

We shared the clinical material at Baragwanath hospital with my white colleagues, but I could not join them for the sessions at the Johannesburg Hospital (white patients exclusively), where the professorial teams worked. So again, I encountered a continuation or replica of the Wits set up, namely segregated and certainly unequal guidance. As a registrar one taught juniors and gave orders. In this regard I had no problems. During my six years at Baragwanath, the atmosphere of especially isolation, improved gradually as more African graduates from the Natal Medical School came through. All of them stayed only for the required one year.

My appointment as the first African registrar in any department at Baragwanath, a somewhat prestigious position, was regarded as a historic event, especially by the predominantly black nursing and clinical and clerical staff. There was perceptible excitement. The nurses organised a public celebratory function, to which my Soweto based relatives, my wife and friends were invited. The occasion was a great success. I am by nature not a gifted speech maker, but on this occasion I tried my best. I even had the courage to relate how my wife had been one of the ten thousand marchers against women's passes in august 1956 when six months pregnant with my first child. The ploy was also to smudge the 1961 scandal reported in the lay press as "a wife who boiled over". I was now a highly respected trainee specialist.

Mokhobo and third wife on his right and colleague and his wife,
at Achievement Award (both doctors received Life Time Achieve Awards)

Teaching clinical medicine was a joy. I fell in love with academic medicine. This joy somehow insulated me against the discomfort of the daily train trips from Benoni station and a Putco bus trip from Johannesburg city, near Park station. There were frequent uncalled for skirmishes between us and the white ticket sellers at Benoni station, a case of insolent and rude whites behaviour against "parmantige" (stubborn) Bantus, who rightly demanded to be served in good time and in a manner that does not create an avoidable stampede as the train arrives. The ripples of the Sharpeville massacre of 1961 were part of the problem. Even at Baragwanath, one sensed some coldness between white staff (doctors and some senior clerks) and black nurses. I believe part of the aura about my celebratory function had to do with interracial covert tension. The routine rudeness became the norm and the white fools at the station were to be ignored most times. For a long time, I was the first and last African registrar in any department, a dejavu to the Bantu Secondary school days for me.

Overnight accommodation was provided for on call work, as well as weekends. On weekends, I preferred to spend time with family and take calls from home, but came Sunday and Saturday mornings for ward rounds. My salary went to a maximum of R120.00 per month as a senior registrar, being 60% of white colleague's, with no transport or other allowance or perks. I was permanently temporary. In the registrar's rotation system, there was a scramble for the best teaching firm head. I was bypassed a few times, but eventually got into this powerful firm of ward 16 and passed my Fellowship examination in 1966. This was another first in my unchartered path of destiny. There was a Dr Machupe Mphahlele who was busy with postgraduate work in the United Kingdom, in gynaecology and obstetrics. He was subsequently to acquire registrable qualifications with the South African Medical Council shortly after me, as he had to earn such in the country.

The East Rand, especially Benoni and Springs attracted an increasing number of African general practitioners. Almost all preferred solo practices. There arose a need to form a fellowship of sorts. For one or other reason, we the pioneers, needed to orientate the new arrivals to the nuances of private practice. It was clear that patients tend to shop around within and between their sought after consultations. Newly arrived doctors were often preferred. This was for a number of beliefs and other reasons. It was believed that new doctors have fresh ideas. Patients also forsook a previous regular doctor because they owed him/her. There also often existed some evaluation of doctors in terms of better knowledge of certain diseases. In our partnership practice, Dumisani Mzamane was said to be better with women's problems and I was better with children. In general, general practitioners would have many common issues to discuss.

It was with a number of thoughts that I invited all doctors in the East Rand to a meeting at Lionel Kent centre, Daveyton. Dr Mzamane agreed to help and we provided entertainment for free at this first meeting. The message reached Soweto and Drs Motlana and Jivhuho came. An idea was unanimously accepted to form The South African Medical Discussion Group (SAMDG), an innocuous apolitical name. As a fulltime employee, I had enough time to run the organisation and prepare academic topics. The organisation blossomed and became popular. It continued even after my self imposed exile to Swaziland in 1969. It subsequently became an organ for fundraising and awarded interest free scholarships to a number of students to study at Natal Medical School. It was dissolved shortly after 1994. Some of its members played a role in the formation of NAMDA, which chose a clear political agenda. The SAMDG was known to the extent that one Professor H W Snyman requested to come address us on the government's intentions about Medunsa (Medical University of Southern Africa, so called). We rejected the concept of half baked African doctors, in a move aimed at closing the now prosperous Natal Medical School to Africans in pursuance of the policy to divide even the "non-whites". The hidden agenda was also to support the Bantustan concept. We saw through this, as did one or two homeland leaders. The SAMDG filled in an important academic role also. The Medical Association of South Africa (MASA), to which some African doctors like myself belonged, failed us in this regard (academic updates). MASA meetings were consistently held at venues where multi-racial gatherings were taboo. The only advantage in being a MASA member was to get the BMJ (British Medical Journal) at a discount. The overall benefit of the SAMDG was to provide a platform where doctors talked to one another. They formed loose partnerships, arranged locum tenens among themselves and came to know private practice and appreciate the reality of healthy competitiveness. The patients' shopping around did not get the doctors to make an issue of the habit.

The Unchartered Journey Hits a Wall

I obtained the Specialist Physician status, satisfied all requirements for registration as such. My ambition was to progress up the maturation ladder as an academic and obtain full qualifications as a Cardiologist. I was inspired by three Clinical Cardiologists, two of whom emigrated (Drs Chesler and Tabatznik). I admired my chief, Leo Schamroff, a world renowned ECGs guru. From my reading I got attracted to the emerging interventional cardiology field and hoped to launch myself from my base, Baragwanath Hospital. The political simmerings were now mainly underground. Many brave African doctors were emigrating, especially to Canada. To add to my deep disappointment, the TPA (Transvaal Provincial Administration) informed me that there were "as yet no permanent posts for Bantu Specialists"! What a blow I felt. I was now a misfit, a pioneer whose progress was never guaranteed. I had run out of lucky breaks. So, I postponed to register, and went back to Daveyton to my old practice. Dr Mzamane took me back, as Dr Dalamba joined the exiles movement to Canada.

I was back to square one socially and as far as local politics were concerned.

A Further Impetus to Change Course

Back in the location business of Daveyton, I was the same old PAC adherent, community advisor and a Specialist Physician working as a glorified general practitioner. My political movements, though muted and cautious, were attracting too much attention. This, I was informed by my special branch patients. Mr Godfrey Pitje was my regular companion in the open, an ANC man, but not an activist. He pursued his private law practice in Johannesburg.

Mrs Thelma Masemola, my sister-in-law, elder sister to my wife came to seek medical help for severe hypertension. She was allowed legally into the country and consulted a Physician, one Dr Lang in Pretoria. She stayed with us. It was believed that the danger person was her husband who was in exile, an ANC member, and that she being a mere wife, was neither on the wanted list nor "quarantined". However, the early hours in July 1967, a posse of SBs under one Blackie Swart (well known and feared SB man), raided my house. We were rudely woken up, interrogated for hours and my house ransacked. Blackie Swart seemed to enjoy going through my personal library, but found nothing to incriminate me. Mrs Masemola was however, collected and locked up, illness not withstanding. She was suspected of having come into the country under false pretences. Her extensive interrogation explored the possibility that she had come on some underground ANC mission. The whole exercise came to naught, after Dr Lang had produced also medical evidence that she had serious hypertension. She was released and she returned to rejoin her husband in exile.

My interest in general practice was waning fast. In fact, I quit and faced the situation of being jobless. Most importantly, I felt vulnerable, increasingly isolated as most of my comrades were either in prison or in exile. I just got up one morning, packed sufficient personal belongings, bundled my family into two cars with some cash in pounds hidden under the car seats and headed for Botswana. Luckily we had travel documents. I had a six months passport issued when I went to the United Kingdom to write the British specialist examinations in 1968. The process had been facilitated by a friend who was a chief clerk in the local office and the location superintendent had recommended. Of course, I had to pay 250 pounds security for the passport and got refunded when I handed it back on my return. My brother-in-law inherited my improved match box structure in Daveyton. Dr Mzamane had also decided to relinquish general practice and Dr Phineas Nene took over.

I literally languished in Gaborone for a month with the kind help of a Dr Simon Moeti and his wife, Dr Nolwandle Mashalaba. They had left their general practice in Kwa-Thema, Springs, two past years and joined the Botswana government service. We all hoped that the permanent secretary for health would fall for my high qualifications, but it was not to be. This man was a British expatriate. Many of these, in differing fields of service in these African countries were known to protect their turf jealously, especially if they felt threatened by the better qualified ex-south Africans.

Swaziland had also acquired independence in 1968. Dr Allen Nxumalo was appointed minister of health. He got to know about my plight and immediately summoned me. My lucky breaks had resurfaced. The journey to somewhere re-started, albeit not quite the route I would have chosen had I had a choice. I was also nursing an additional disappointment if not bitterness in my deep heart, in that I did not get a chance to go back to Scotland to re-write the second part of the MRCP. I do not know what I wanted to do with this prestigious diploma. After all, I had the equally prestigious FCP (SA). I guess, I was a bundle of frustrations for social, political and professional reasons, but kept outward healthy signs and managed somehow to function.

THE JOURNEY IN THE WILDERNESS STARTS: A RURAL MEDICAL SPECIALIST ROUTE

It is 1969; I arrive bag and baggage in scenic beautiful Swaziland. I am very warmly received and made to feel like a VIP. The excitement of Uhuru is infectious and much enviable. We move into a spacious government house on the hospital premises. There is no difficulty in getting my children into good schools, one at Waterford, two into Mbabane. The hospital environment is jovial, the average Swazi citizen is very friendly and I find many South Africans, mainly teachers, all very happy socially and in their jobs. Among these, I found to my surprise, PAC comrades and other former acquaintances from Fort Hare. We were shortly joined by other South African doctors, recruited by Dr Nxumalo. Among them was a former neighbour at Benoni, Dr Ellen Blekie and her journalist husband. The work at the main hospital, Mbabane Government Hospital became challenging, and interesting. It was a strange experience for one coming from Baragwanath. To describe the facilities as minimally basic is an understatement. My work was expected to cover anything, as there was a severe shortage of medical staff. In fact, I was shocked when I was regarded as a type of "General Specialist "for children and adults! This turned out to be another "first" for me. The first ever specialist in any medical discipline in the Kingdom of Swaziland! Expectations were high. Shortages were all round, nursing, support staff, doctors, drugs, and more than basic diagnostic facilities.

This was a daunting challenge, calling for much innovation. Outside internal medicine proper, I learned anew to give general anaesthesia, whenever I could. There were good general practitioners who provided guidance. These white doctors, included South African missionaries and British expatriates. Those who practiced in the surgical specialities were self taught and quite good. I got quite extended in due course, as a preferred doctor to royalty, prominent Swazi politicians and fellow South Africans. I adapted and learned to improvise and innovate in order to function despite shortages of sometimes very basic items. I got accustomed to a common response to a request, "kute dokotela" (none doctor), as a nurse nonchalantly throws up her arms, as if it was the accepted norm. I then proceeded as best as I could. For example, I would economise on dialysis fluid by leaving it longer in the peritoneal cavity than the conventional time. In other innovative methods, I would decrease dosages and or lengthen dosage intervals of medicines. Deciding on empiric treatments on minimal criteria was common. One realised how patients can do well in spite of what is done or not done!

Human blood was a special rare commodity. On several occasions, one was called to theatre to assist with auto-transfusion, giving back the patient's blood removed from the abdomen in the case of a ruptured pregnancy, a practice that would please Jehovah's Witnesses. The writing of patients' clinical notes on the small cards used as patients' files required a special skill of writing legibly in small letters, squeezing details into the available space, ensuring that sense would be made of the information at subsequent follow up. Optimal efficient medical practice in an under-resourced Southern African environment was a pleasant challenge indeed.

I started the process of task shifting in order to lighten the burden and to deliver good care. I personally taught and trained nurses in clinical medicine, with surprising success. This also included teaching any suitable person to put up drips, take bloods, doing ECG. I had fortunately brought along my own personal ECG machine. The hospital had none. Unfortunately X-ray films were dried up in the sun, resulting in smudging. They were of reasonable quality, but I decided to see these whilst wet and dripping watery development solution.

One of highlights was the advent of the Harry's Angels programme. The monthly visits by the teams from Johannesburg, of specialists led by a radiologist, Dr David Cohen, was a welcome breeze of medical civilisation.

The programme was financed by Mr Harry Oppenheimer, as a humanitarian gesture for free to the Kingdom. It was academically satisfying and a privilege to be part of the mercy trips. I selected suitable cases for locally doable interventions, diagnostic or therapeutic, and provide after care after they have left. Some of the novel procedures I witnessed included, Air encephalogram, burr holes and closed mitral valvulotomy for tight mitral stenosis. I must state with pride that many an accurate diagnosis was made with sound basic clinical skill, judgement, and a modicum of basic investigations. Mis-judgements were rare.

My stay in Swaziland was socially and professional satisfying, but felt uncertain of being permanently acceptable. There were a fair number of South Africans, mostly teachers. This provided some comfort, but never a sense of belonging. Besides there was also here as in Botswana, a notion that the British expatriates regarded any educated south African as a threat and used any trick to influence the locals against creating for such a foreigner a feeling of permanence and ferment negative sentiments. Yes, there were enjoyable social amenities which we were denied by the apartheid system. You could enjoy a good time, have an alcoholic drink without fear and play golf on a proper course. At this time at home we played golf on sand greens with no fairways laid out. The Jew owned courses would allow the natives to play on their courses on Christmas day. However, there was this culture shock. This came in various forms. There was the language, the local mores and the British colonialist's manoeuvres to survive as long as is possible post independence, by fanning anti-black South African feelings. In fact, we were shocked when a friend, Mr Layton Plata was ruthlessly evicted from Swaziland through lies. He was accused of being a South African informer.

At some stage, I felt compelled to engineer some hope of acceptance. I heard that one could sign up allegiance to a village chief to show your bonafides as an African intent on becoming a citizen and identifying with the local people. The system was called "uku khonta". It was a primitive progress of going to some meeting, sit on the floor, be seen and acknowledged in an informal manner. I did not feel that this traditional method, without some written legal backing, would secure a future for my children. It was a weird experience that would guarantee nothing. The last straw was when the King's government passed a law which effectively closed the door to citizenship even for children of foreigners who would be born in Swaziland. My streak of lucky breaks seemed to be ending. I had hit another brick wall on the promise of a journey to somewhere even on this detour. The permanent secretary for health in Lesotho, Dr Lepoqo Molapo threw bait to me during one of the many intercountry deliberations between the two countries. We met at cocktail party, to many of which I was always invited as a VIP. I was certainly captivated by his smooth talk. Besides, it sounded like the barriers obtaining in Swaziland would be minimal. The language is familiar, the culture could be assumed to be near ones own. It felt also that my children will be able to continue with their schooling, as some Basotho children were attending the good schools in Swaziland, especially the very popular Waterford Kamhlaba, founded by Mr Michael Stern. This man had quit his post as headmaster of the famous St Peter's High School, where he had had tremendous success.

The Bantu Education System was gaining a stronger foot hold and Mike Stern procured funds to establish Waterford and continue top class education for Africans and, in addition, encompasses a multi-racial schooling environment for south Africans, even though freedom did not seem to be that near. Many outstanding African South African intellectuals, subsequent leaders and politicians were products of the renowned St Peters High School.

LESOTHO, 1971

My family left for Lesotho on our travel documents. It my mother, my wife and the youngest child who was not yet at boarding school. We were aware of the serious political problems in Lesotho after the latest elections, but we were optimistic. I was approached through a personal visit by King Sobhuza the second himself, to the utter amazement of even the Swazi citizen. He unsuccessfully tried to persuade me to change my mind by offering Swazi citizenship at this late hour. He brought the written document, duly signed by him. This was touching. I did not know that I was that much appreciated. I knew I was the physician to royalty, but this belated gesture was almost overwhelming. I politely but vaguely promised that I may come back, as I accepted the certificate with gratitude. However, I recall that there was a subsequent law passed, which nullified my citizenship. I came to know about this when I decided to sell a small free hold plot I had bought.

Swaziland was poorly resourced yes, but Lesotho was destitute in many respects regarding health facilities. The country had just emerged from a major political turmoil following the recent elections, a background that added its own dimension to the social and health problems.

The reception for me and my family was the warmest ever, really superb. The local language was familiar. My mother felt particularly at home. I was soon told of a village around Maseru, Khubetsoana, under one Chief Mokhobo. I had the pleasure of meeting him, paid my respects and a few sittings exchanging information. However, his tribe used a completely different totem from ours. But it was comforting to know the Lesotho Mokhobos, especially of royalty, and one vaguely nurtured a possibility of permanent settlement in the country. I felt very much at home as I met a number of basothos, whom one had regarded as South Africans. These had returned to reclaim Lesotho citizenship to escape the harsh apartheid regime. In fact one or two had skipped the border running from arrest; one in particular had been temporarily imprisoned for ANC activities. There was also a number of refugees from South Africa some of whom I knew.

The future socially and politically held promise of happy home. I was captivated by the infectious laughter of the indigenous people, their very loud conversing style even at close range. The dry mountains, devoid of vegetation had their own distinctive beauty. We adapted to the seeming inconvenience of having to cross the border to do shopping of even basic items. Such trips to Ladybrand or Bloemfontein about hundred and fifty kilometres away were enjoyable. One could afford to tolerate the invariable uncalled for hostile reception and harassment on the South African side of the border post. There was, however an odd feeling that Lesotho was like home, even though politically you felt more vulnerable than in Swaziland. There was Mozambique to the east of Swaziland, which created a sense of security, should the apartheid regime clamp down. There was the expected shortage of staff, medicines and poor supportive facilities. Basic drugs ran out regularly, and a consignment of WHO donated supplies did provide relief, though antibiotics were either expired or about to. We used them nevertheless, in the absence of anything else and the patients got better.

THE RURAL SPECIALIST CONTINUES TO SURVIVE

Innovation, compromise and a safe breaking of the conventional forms of medical treatment again became the order of my practice. However, the environment at the main hospital, Maseru was a welcome improvement on the Mbabane set up. There was good professional company, at least. There was a Mosotho neuro-psychiatrist, trained in the United Kingdom, the first such, in fact, in southern Africa, a Wits graduate, Dr Victor Ntshekhe. There was an expatriate Specialist Surgeon, a citizen of India, who was also trained in the U.K. The specialist team was completed by a South African trained gynaecologist, who was also the permanent secretary for health, joined shortly after by another gynaecologist, a citizen of Lesotho, trained in Durban and had been my class mate at Fort Hare in first year B.Sc. The specialist numbers grew pretty fast, as an Israel trained Opthalmologist arrived and another Lesotho citizen, a Psychiatrist trained in UK arrived with his wife who had had some basic training at diploma level in paediatrics.

The pioneer Physician was in good company. There was much improvement in academic life, with a great deal of discussions, and regular joint meetings. Among the general practitioners on the hospital staff, was Dr. Luthuli-Ngakane, the daughter of Chief Albert Luthuli, the immediate past president of the ANC. She was a joy to interact with and exuded a strange hope for us that freedom may not be hat far after all. There were also a couple South African trained general practitioners in private practice.

Among the highlight developments, was the formation of the first Lesotho Medical Association and Medical Council, in which I served and was one of the founders thereof. I established the Lesotho Medical Journal and was the sole Editor. My re-connection with academic life continued on a high note, as I single-handedly organised the first ever Lesotho Medical Congress! One felt resurrected indeed. I invited a number of South African Physicians, among them my teachers and contemporaries at Baragwanath hospital, and they obliged. The advertisement of the congress also attracted a Physician from Bloemfontein, Dr J R Kriel and his friend, Dr Louw Olivier. These two, were to play another role in my professional life a few years later.

One was totally insulated against the problems of scarce medical resources. In fact, I more than just survived. I published in my journal and in the South African Medical Journal. My work still required sound clinical skills with a modicum of what extra-clinical support was available. The load was manageable, especially with delegated skills, that I undertook to teach to my subordinates, much like in Swaziland. The spectrum of clinical cardiac pathology differed somewhat between the two countries. In Lesotho, hypertension was commoner, as was diabetes and idiopathic dilated cardiomyopathy. The seeming interesting connection between hypertension and dilated cardiomyopathy, I got to publish in the East African Medical Journal. Rheumatic Heart Disease was rare, surprisingly. In Swaziland I had published as well, a few times in the South African Medical Journal. I had a skirmish with Dr Von Biljon, the editor, when he insisted I change the designation "African" to "bantu" before accepting my article. I did conform, but used designations "bantu" and "non-bantu" in place of African and white. The article, comparative postulate on attitudes, was published! The editor missed the humour!

Lesotho was more Africa orientated and intellectually open north wards. Therefore one had an opportunity to meet East African visiting Physicians. A somewhat firmer connection with home occurred happily. Anton Rupert, the tobacco manufacturing giant, set up a similar humanitarian flying doctor service to that of Swaziland, Anton Rupert's Angels.

The Anton Rupert's Angels of mercy operated locally successfully. The commonest locally operable condition was constrictive pericarditis, most likely post-tuberculous. Cases were diagnosed and chosen without a single mistake, on basic clinical data, chest X-ray and ECG. There was no recourse to an invasive investigative procedure. In any case this was not available. After some time a small "real time" echocardiogram machine was acquired and was extra help. But, even before this happy development, a number of pericardiocentesis procedures had been successfully and safely performed. The close similarities between pericarditis and dilated cardiomyopathy was never a stumbling block.

I established a commendable reputation especially as a Physician to His Majesty's household and to political heavy weights. The secretary for health offered me a year's WHO scholarship to Denmark in 1973. Being such a valued physician, I was lent a temporary passport, a gesture facilitated easily, albeit an "illegal" gesture. I was thus one of a dozen third world cardiologists who gained valuable experience in interventional cardiology, a technical expertise at its infancy at the time. In this way, I was academically reborn, my dream fulfilled. I also had a chance to witness the health services in the Scandinavian countries. The wonderful bonus was when I met some of my former comrades in exile. We caught up on many issues abroad and I filled them on home issues as best as I could recall. This was another memorable part of the journey in the wilderness, possibly a little promise of "going somewhere", though not much was yet visible in the horizon.

A feeling of uncertainty continued to nag me. Happily on my return from Denmark nothing happened when I touched down at the Johannesburg airport. I had fears that I would be detained and possible face harassing interrogation as I met political refugees abroad and socialised a lot. I had some persons following me even to the London airport. South African spies were known to be ubiquitous.

Much was done to make us feel at home in Lesotho. However, lacking was some modern legal backing that I knew of, that would guarantee me or my children citizenship, and South Africa was too close for comfort. With the development of some family and personal problems, and all my children having finished or about to complete high school, I decided to look for greener pastures again as my contract expired. By this time Medunsa had taken off with or without the support of the disadvantaged majority. I applied for any post in cardiology or internal medicine. The reply was a terse statement that there were no posts for bantu specialists yet. I could not believe the arousal of the sense of déjà vu! The road to somewhere had to be re-negotiated, and comes a lucky break from an unpredicted source. A number of my patients from Daveyton had followed me to Swaziland. One notable person in this group was Chief Mangope, who afforded to follow me Lesotho as well. So at our chance meeting, hearing my uncertainties, he invited me Bophutatswana, at that stage, a self-governing homeland. The bait for me was a safe return via Botswana. So I accepted and flew to Gaborone, then motor to Mafikeng as a chaperoned VIP.

MAFIKENG, BOPHUTATSWANA, 1975

Mokhobo, second wife, and their young daughters at Mafikeng hospital house
(Hospital superintendent, physician, minister of health 1979-1985)

I was now a bachelor, alone and lonesome. My children's university studies were arranged, but I also needed more money to provide for their needs. My salary in Mafikeng was by comparison to the expatriate salary in Lesotho was very generous and I was also now given extra perks. Soon I got married a second time to a social worker and subsequently had two daughters. My wife transferred from Bloemfontein and joined my department of health and social welfare.

We got temporary accommodation in a village close to the homeland's main hospital, Bophelong Hospital. The superintendent of the hospital was a missionary, Dr Jan Richter. There were interns and one Psychiatrist. I was put in charge of the medical section as Principal Specialist. The hospital had 900 beds, 70% of the patients were for chronic psychiatry care. My task as the Physician was to develop the medical section and decrease the psychiatry patients. Chief Mangope, as head of a "self governing" state, preparing for "independence" soon, wielded much power already. He moved us from the primitive environment at Lomanyaneng village and accommodated us in the garage at the Commissioner-Generals premises. This was a little more habitable, but still primitive. The nursing staffs at Bophelong were predominantly black, under a white matron. The administrative and supportive staff was predominantly white, conservative Afrikaners. There were separate tea rooms, and toilets. The latter clearly indicated use by bantu males and bantu females. The car parking area also designated areas mainly by status. Mine was for a "Psycian", as the white work shop man, a jovial Mnr Wium, had not been given the correct spelling of this strange animal. The head office personnel was mixed, and the secretary for health was a white missionary doctor, whose wife was the Chief nursing officer. The Director of health services was a liberal Afrikaner, a Specialist Physician, Dr J R Kriel, whom I had met in Maseru at thy conference I had organised. We renewed acquaintances and became close friends.

Chief Mangope moved fairly swiftly on many fronts, pre-independence. Three comfortable houses were built in the hospital area for senior black staff, including me. There was, however, still strict separation with a tall wall separating our three houses from the many white dwellings. It was like Baragwanath Hospital again. We meet in the wards, come to the superintendent's meetings together, have separate tea breaks and "separate but equal" residential places for blacks and whites. The pioneer Physician, on the road to somewhere proceeded to convert a psychiatric hospital to a general hospital, with minimum medical manpower. This was quite an adventure. Dr Kriel invades the hospital, pulls down derogatory toilet notices and forcibly "integrates" tea drinking. Mr Mangope appoints the first Physician of the territory, medical superintendent. Dr Richter leaves. The general section gets recognised by the Medical Council for more interns, as it is now fairly well run. I experiment with integrated disciplines, because of staff shortage. Departing from the conventional system, I designated disciplines as "cutting" or "non-cutting", in addition to division by gender and age.

The nursing staff, administrative and supportive staff increased through almost exclusively black appointees. The complexion of the institution had literally changed by the time "independence" happened in 1979. There was an inflow of black interns as well, some of them homeland bursary holders. The hospital conversion process, though daunting, had gotten underway quickly. The hotch potch of psychiatric patients, many of whom had been just dumped were dispatched by any means possible. A surprisingly large number of them were from outside South Africa. When independence came, the general hospital had the majority beds, senior posts were occupied by blacks, especially nursing and administrative. Many white staff either left on their own accord or were replaced (africanisation). The Physician-Superintendent broke down the wall of separation and moved to a bigger house on the "white" side, very spacious facility, which was previously occupied by an unmarried psychiatrist.

The hospital indeed prospered. The Director of health services, who had angrily torn down the offending notices and forcibly integrated the multi-racial staff, joined as a second Physician at the hospital. Interns were of all races, from various medical schools. In fact a community much happier than "across the border", blossomed. Senior medical staff was recruited from East Africa, mainly Ugandan refugees, but also from West Africa, as well as missionaries from Europe. Later, Israel entered into an exchange programme for doctors and other personnel in other government departments. The independent state registered the recruited foreign doctors on its own medical register formulated by the Department of Health. The facilities also improved to a satisfactory level, even looking like luxury compared to the two countries I previously worked in. The prosperity, however, sabotaged my previous ambition of borderless disciplines and establishment of progressive medical care and a cluster system of disciplines. The conventional disciplines of surgical, medical, gynaecological, paediatric and psychiatric sections, returned. Primary Health care and the principles of Alma Ata were, however, soon vigorously pursued. A new strategy of health care deliver was evolved.

The rural Specialist and hospital superintendent decided to accept co-option into the cabinet as Minister of Health with the label of a technocrat. The homeland was now independent. The language of independence sounded good, as there was talk of the step being one to greater independence in the not too distant future. A further reason for taking the bait of overall head of health and policy maker, was the realisation that the health department's top brass had somewhat stagnated. These people were inexperienced and professionally junior. They were ex-missionaries who did share my views on primary health care. I was very enthused with this direction, having been a rural specialist long enough to see the need and took up the challenge. In many ways Bophutatswana was socio-economically not very different from the two countries I have just come from. I was a minister who continued to keep a firm hand in clinical practice, hands on type of leadership. I led by example to implement the Alma Ata philosophy, as I recognised it as the answer to the prevailing health needs.

Staff was an obvious problem. Permanent doctors, mainly recruits from outside South Africa, were improving the situation at the main hospital. The challenge was to decentralise services, and organise a network of clinics of different levels of care and ensure adequate facilities, sufficient manpower and take the consumer public along, away from a hospi-centric culture. To this end, community health committees were established and orientated. Health education was introduced, offered by properly orientated, suitably supervised community members.

The scheme was to generate confidence of the people in the clinics. By some stroke of luck, a few Batswanas had gone to Uganda to study as health educators. It was therefore easy to complement their numbers gradually. Together with this task, I undertook to delegate more responsibilities to nurses trained as nurse clinicians. The minister cum superintendent cum Specialist Physician took up the cudgels to produce nurse practitioners, single handedly. He deviced the syllabus and wrote the teaching manuals. The clinics, the hospital outpatient department, and casualty, were manned by competent nurse practitioners. Their scope included clinical practice and management which encompassed broad health education. The minister authorised nurses to prescribe by issuing appropriate standing orders. I subsequently invited Professor Lucy Wagstaff of Wits and Baragwanath hospital to help with the paediatric component on weekends. She helped at no direct remuneration. Accommodation only, was provided. The course was so highly successful, that it was subsequently adopted by the S A Nursing council under Professor Charlotte Searle as an official certificated qualification.

The Bophutatswana health Experiment flourished and was acclaimed by many, in other homelands and in South Africa. Courage and a driving Africanist spirit to do the best under the circumstances for the disadvantaged masses, had paid off. Illness could not wait for greater independence to be addressed.

The programme kept me very busy and was also a welcome distraction from the cabinet meetings. On the few occasions I attended these, I felt uncomfortable. There were arguments and discussions which made feel a total misfit. In fact, I would come out of these meetings feeling as if I had sold out on my political beliefs. A few episodes lifted my spirits. One was my trip to Kimberly to see ailing Robert Sobukwe in Kimberly. He was accommodated at my father in law's house. I really came back feeling resurrected. The occasional ANC recruit en route to Botswana, as arranged telephonically with Dr Motlana, passed through my house to have refreshments and survey the safety of the onward journey. I even had occasion to chaperon at much risk, a comrade and homeboy, Peter Lehola, in exile in London, who came through the Botswana border, went to Potchefstroom to see his family. He successfully slipped out before the Special Branch got hint of his whereabouts. These refreshing events gave me steam to "Africanise" mission hospitals. My heart was with the innocent majority, for whom a quality health service had to be offered regardless of the location. So, previous mission hospitals were renamed, functionally re-organised along the primary health care system and the nurse practitioner programme expanded. Bophelong hospital was the training centre. All hospitals had to support the satellite clinics through regular doctor visits, re-enforced with a directive to promote community participation and health education. Extra help came in various forms, in the health and social welfare departments. The Minister of Health buttressed his vision with legislation where appropriate. Dr J R Kriel, my Director of Health services was a valued ally as we shared the same views. An Anti-smoking Act was passed, a measure that raised consternation in the mind of Mr Anton Rupert. A gesture of interest, facilitated by the President of the homeland, was my being flown to Stellenbosch in private jet. The exercise was designed to convince me through counter propaganda that tobacco was not as harmful. I was shown written evidence by other experts in this regard. I was not impressed and the Act became law. The banning of smoking was to apply to indoors as well as at stadiums, a very ambitious objective.

The political irritations and distractions were many, but a bulwark was my professional integrity and sincere ambition to implement primary health care. I totally rejected the idea of a medical school, whilst Transkei established one. My programme consisted of establishing satellite clinics. Only one hospital was built, at Lehurutshe. The architectural design had to reflect that this was a referral centre in a network of facilities for delivering primary health care. It was to function in a District Health Service manner. A missionary doctor, committed colleague, Dr Meyer agreed to be the head.

At the main hospital, the minister kept a firm hand in clinical medicine. A non-medical medical superintendent was appointed and the experiment was highly successful. The minister's role was to teach interns, run the medical section, train nurse clinicians, and use the trained nurses to train others. The scope was that of a Physician between a regional and tertiary hospital. There were facilities and staff for dialysis, mainly peritoneal, especially emergencies. B y arrangement with a Baragwanath nephrologist, my former general practice partner, Dr D V A Mzamane, one or two patient had arterio-venous shunts done. Where suitable, permanent peritoneal catheters were inserted locally. There were regular academic meetings and clinical discussions. For a long time the passion for interventional cardiology was shelved. The work at hand was challenging enough.

There was much by way of medical surgical procedures anyway, such as organ biopsies and therapeutic serous effusions removal. Unfortunately for my colleagues, my dream and my patients, the political environment became progressively difficult to tolerate. I found it uncomfortable to play schizophrenic pretences. Political interference compromised my administrative style. It was embarrassing to meet a member of staff in the street, for example, who was dismissed without my knowledge and for unacceptable reasons. I clashed with the head of state on many decisions relating to promotion of staff in both the health and social welfare sections. These were mainly permanent nurses, administrative personnel and social workers. Even in our dealings with advisors and with aid from Israel and the United Kingdom, my chief and I had antagonistic styles. I grew restless, and worried about my independence and professional integrity. My true political mindset came to the fore and I started agonising about the perceived local status in the context of the greater South African situation. The events that had occurred by this time, the Soweto students uprising, the Lesotho raids, (where my children were still schooling), the death of Sobukwe and Steve Biko, took their toll on my conscience. I wondered if this was not a time to look at an unlucky break rather than a lucky one in order for my destiny to change course. My initial naive rationale perhaps, that the innocent majority must have the best possible health care in transition to true independence needed a closer analysis. I had countered criticisms from my comrades in South Africa with the belief that it was mandatory to provide health care regardless. I remembered how Dr Motlana among others, had labelled this homeland Mangopeland. The Daveyton memories came to haunt me also, surprisingly. I remembered how Dr William Nkomo's ASSECA had, in a sense, provided a better political cushion there. This was an organisation I had joined. Its focus was on social and educational "emancipation" of Africans from the hard core oppression intellectually, and look at ways to address poverty. In fact, conceptually, this was a softened forerunner to Biko's Black Consciousness philosophy. We espoused black pride and self sufficiency in things doable (vukasenzele).

After what I regard as the longest six years of my entire life, I resigned. The last straw, was when the cabinet endorsed an illogical persecution of Mr Joe Seremane, who was simply mobilising the local community to form an organised voice against oppression. And oppression existed, plus corruption, plus nepotism. It was shocking to realise how a majority "cabinet" decision, binding as it was when it comes into the open, was committing. There was a collective stance, regardless of whatever minority view there could have been. An Israeli doctor, a friend, could not believe that a person can be "blinded" by integrity to that extent that he jumps ship a "poor" man, when others have acquired businesses and farms at no cost. But I departed with my conscience and integrity intact and held my head high. My wife continued working. We were more comfortable as she was no more the intensely disliked Minister's wife, who was not docile like others or appear to worship the system. My daughters were at very good local schools. There was a silver lining to the darkness of Bantustanism in Bophuthatswana. The efforts to appear to be genuinely independent extended to the establishment of good schools. There was even an International school, which enrolled children from Botswana.

MAFIKENG'S FIRST PHYSICIAN SPECIALIST

Setting up private practice, which my only choice for now, was a way survival with an unknown tomorrow. It was also a blind pioneering jump in my now very chequered path. This was an unintended fulfilment of a rural specialist profile. One source of delight that lit up my spirits, was when Professor Louw Olivier, Head of Cardiology at Medunsa appointed me part time lecturer. What a lifeline it was! I was sad to leave Bophelong hospital permanently though. The hospital had prospered, become popular with interns and other career doctors. Primary health care in the homeland was a marvel for any one to appreciate.

In fact the concept had been exported to other parts of third world Southern Africa. There were frequent meetings among homeland health ministers and there was one or two publications by my team. A private hospital came into being in town, Victoria Hospital, seemingly the market existed. However, for the time I was in Mafikeng, I did not have occasion to use the facility.

The Specialist private practice as a pioneer Physician was a challenge. My signage had to be specific and boldly spell out the type of cases I would see and which ones not. My clientele included all racial groups, with a surprising number of Afrikaans speaking old tannies from as Zeerust. There were patients who came from, Botswana and the far Western Transvaal and nearby conservative towns. News seemed to have spread fast. There was, however, an occasional stray maternity case or a desperate mother with a baby. The trauma cases included victims of torture in the hands of the security police. These would consist of electric burns, shambok bruises or some young man who survived suffocation when a sack was tied over his head in an effort to extract information. Dr Motlana and I were in communication whenever a contingent of young comrades had boarded transport in Soweto. I had the privilege of caring for the wife of Mr Joe Mathews and her family that had come down from Botswana. We also enjoyed a resurgence of the true spirit of independence in the new Mahikeng surburb. A group of my wife's friend bravely celebrated Mandela's birthday.

A useful distraction, academically refreshing, was my trip to Medunsa as part time lecturer in the department of cardiology, 1985-1989. I subsequently joined the department on a full time basis 1990, January, just before Mr Mandela was released. By the end of 1989, I reflected on the mixture of joy, pain, frustration, unfulfilled ambitions when still young enough, and the disadvantages or otherwise of pioneering without any prior preparation. I felt I had along the way been thrust into one or other situation. On the rural specialist path, certainly much of my true academic and professional armamentarium had been lost. I was touched by the compliments in Dr George Cohen's article (British Museum Journal, 1972, (4) pp288-290) and Bob Hitchcock's book, Harry's Angels. The references to my potential were generous.

In the journey as chequered, something had also to crack up. My first marriage had collapsed. Fortunately my three children in this relationship did well, having obtained university bursaries eventually after initial sponsorship by my pocket. The Lesotho connection was useful in this regard. They all studied and completed outside South Africa. They came to visit me in Mafikeng, and returned to settle in Johannesburg after Mandela's release.

I was on the second marriage in Mafikeng. On my relocation to Johannesburg, my younger daughter enrolled at a private school in Pretoria and the older had won a Rotary scholarship to Canada. She was soon to study at the University of Cape Town.

Mokhobo, second wife, graduation of their second daughter and first daughter

My wife got a good job at Eskom, did well, and was voted Business woman of the year in 1994. We bought a comfortable house in the northern suburbs of Johannesburg, my mother coming to the area as a madam, where she was for many years, a maid. I also re-connected with my relatives in Potchefstroom and made acquaintance with others previously unknown, in Mafikeng. It was of the latter, a Mrs Malebatso who insisted I go to see my biological father in Bothaville. I yielded, we went, but unfortunately Mr Motsemme had passed on. He had no brothers, only two sisters. I traced some cousins of his to the new township of Potchefstroom, as I was searching for some idea as to the kind of genes I have inherited from that side.

MORE ON THE INNER STUFF

Mokhobo lay preacher A M E Church,

All along on the journey to somewhere, the church remained part of me. Every where I went, I would seek and find the African Methodist Episcopal Church. I got on well with every pastor where I chose to worship and held various offices, sometimes more than one where manpower was short. In Mafikeng, I worshipped at the church in the village of Lorwaneng under Chief Setumo Montshiwa. I met him and other elderly batswanas. In my younger days, the pastors of the church were older men

As I grew older, the pastors coming forth are younger than me. Nevertheless, I relate very well with most. When I was minister of health, I had an opportunity to travel widely in Bophutatswana and learned a lot about the Batswana culture. I met Dr Modiri Molema before he died. This was before I settled in Mafikeng. In fact we had a long and interesting discussion in his surgery in the village. I got interested in the history and read his two books, written around barolong chiefs, Moroka and Montshioa. I also gained much insight into the culture as our committee of translations grappled with this task under the leadership of Professor Jack Setshedi.

My inspiration to become a doctor occurred through seeing and hearing Dr Don Cindi (Wits MBBch 1951). He was a friend of Mr S McDover Lekhela, the secondary school principal. He gave regular motivational talks. He was suave, always smartly dressed and spoke good English. I just admired him and nurtured the ambition. Dr A H Bismilla (Wits, MBBch 1949), also contributed to the ambition. He was the first son of Potchefstroom to qualify, and the first non-white to do so. As a general practitioner of colour, he gave a humane and welcome face to the profession at the doorstep of the township, and I felt I could emulate him. The white general practitioners in town had separate rooms for the races, with inferior quality for Africans, who would always be seen last. This also planted further seeds for a career in medicine. Generally, the environment in Potchefstroom was hostile to Africans. After attending a cinema in town, there would always be unprovoked fights between Africans and whites. I was a coward. I kept away from the fights. Even in the township, if a quarrel arose during a gambling game, I would rather leave my money and run home. Generally, the spirit of activism did not grow in me.

I have wondered why Mr Von Abo chose me from among many piccanins on his farm to look after the son, Crawford. My first school teacher in Sub A, Mr Letsie, when he left for Lesotho, he requested that my aunt allow him to adopt me. This was a peculiar request, because I do not think he knew my circumstances. He just took a liking to me. I was one of the foundation members of the Pan Africanist Congress, in 1959. When it came to the allocation of duties, Mr Robert Sobukwe seemed to pity this youthful looking cadre. I was thus assigned a somewhat peripheral and harmless role to head fund raising activities. This "let off", ensured my subsequent gentle treatment by the special branch police. There was always this "something" about me that chartered an inexplicable course. My flirtations with school committees and the school board in Daveyton, and my subsequent flirtations with the homeland politics, contextualised pragmatism and a belief in taking a balanced view of issues before plunging into hard core activism or similar. When many of my contemporaries emigrated abroad, I chose to look for greener pastures near home. I could have been a good professional export material to any western country at the time. This same attitude guided me to join Medunsa when the opportunity presented, forgetting how vehemently I rejected its establishment. I rationalised that it had taken off regardless and that young African minds needed a face to identify with and perhaps a role model. I arrived at Medunsa almost at the sunset of my life, accepted a junior position and focussed on effective delivery. My wanderings and survival in the wilderness as a rural specialist had not stopped me from publishing from there, to maintain some semblance of academic credentials. This little bit stood me in good stead for Medunsa. When Dr Von Biljon, the editor of the SA Medical journal tried to frustrate my humble efforts, I found an avenue in journals in the African hinterland. I published from any location, and found a slot in East and West Africa. Being patient and thick skinned can be a virtue. Pragmatism dictated that any voice from anywhere, no matter how small or liable to be stigmatised, can be a useful lone voice of reason. To move from anywhere to somewhere unobtrusively can be a worthy success.

THE MEDICAL UNIVERSITY OF
SOUTHERN AFRICA (MEDUNSA)

Mokhobo, Minister of Health, 1979-1985

The widely travelled southern African specialist, arrived virtually at the sunset of his life at an acceptable destination. It was a cherished destination, though not the one the ambitious younger man, when at his prime, would have chosen. Yes, one was wiser and richer in experience with third world southern African health environments. I was consoled with the realisation that politically, hopes for the majority was alive during one's life time. The erstwhile despicable unwanted apartheid system was in imminent derailment from its intended purpose. Medunsa had taken off with or without black opinion. Perhaps, there was still room to make some contribution for the democratic system.

The administrative machinery that had rejected the bantu specialist were still in place. Of interest was that at least one department was headed by a bantu specialist, Professor E T Mokgokong, head of gynaecology and obstetrics, who was recruited in 1980. In fact, he had encouraged me to come and was part of the interviewing panel. There were also a few blacks in the middle professional echelons in one or two other departments. Some would sit on the senate.

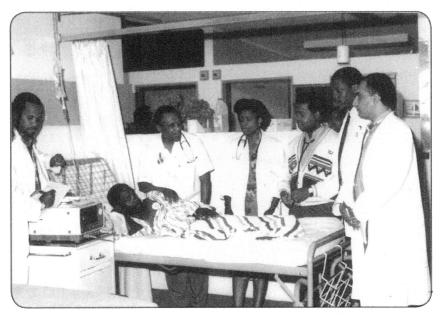

Mokhobo Professor of Cardiology and Internal Medicine

I had this rapid meteoric rise from senior specialist, through Associate Professor of Cardiology to become Head of Medicine and Cardiology in a space of three years. I did feel the general sympathy among African senior staff on my situation, more or less regarded as a senior who had been done down unfairly. The student politics were in turmoil at the time, led by activists, espousing the spirit of African self determination. There was an apparent defiance against the entirely white top hierarchy. I did try and arbitrate as a senior black, at the risk of being regarded as a sell-out or "softy". However, the experience of trying to do so was a good introduction to the mentality of these students at this stage of the country's history. I was older than most lecturers and even white heads of departments. The African staff probably had a third sense about my chequered past which had not been of my making. The openings for promotion were also created by one or other tragedy. Such events, again, shaped the journey in some mysterious way. I settled in quickly, developed my own style of teaching and training students from disadvantaged backgrounds. I realised how the rough journey had equipped me with a unique flavour in style to function inside and outside Medunsa. It was a special pleasure to be wedged into what was a nascent African academic development. This was appropriately consonant with the evolving political changes in the country.

I regarded the challenge being to deliver as teacher, as role model, a black leader and an exponent of African excellence, to disprove the philosophy underpinning some of tenets of the apartheid era.

Despite one or two internal hiccups, I adapted smoothly, and avoided being idealistic. For in my first year as Head of Medicine, I personally failed 30% of the final year students, the highest ever such number. My style of teaching took time to be understood and accepted. It was designed to infuse confidence in a black child, but could and was misunderstood as "giving too little", or condescending or too "simplistic", and expecting too much afterwards. Yet, I knew that it was based on first hand knowledge and insight. My instruction to my staff was that they mark students on content and not language or expression in English. I reassured everyone that this was not to drop standards, but to be realistic. Our students came from diverse disadvantaged backgrounds, for whom English was not the first language, and my innovation was a necessity. I took this attitude to higher levels when I became the Dean of the Faculty of medicine. I believed that everyone matures with time.

As external examiner at other medical schools, with the same attitude, I had no difficulty in projecting my style, in a multi-racial set up or predominantly black student group. At the postgraduate level, however, there was no compromise. All candidates had matured in time and were expected to be equivalent. In fact, ironically, at the postgraduate level for the Fellowship and MMed candidates, I felt guilty of setting unrealistically excessive expectations.

The general environment at Medunsa became very accommodating and enjoyable. One even forgot that there would be retirement soon. Professor Mokgokong went up the ladder as Vice Chancellor, African heads of departments were appointed and middle level professional positions were filled by Africans. The somewhere had become a somewhat definite destination, reached in a manner unplanned. My long cherished ambitions were somewhat revived. I enjoyed serving in the various Colleges of Medicine committees, almost as a given.

I was disappointed that since 1966, when I broke the ice, and for almost thirty years, not much had happened to accelerate the production of African specialists generally. Shortly after me, Dr Nimrod Sishuba followed, and then emigrated. There was a Dr Jolobe who qualified in the United Kingdom as a Physician. There was a little better sprinkle of Specialists in Obstetrics and Gynaecology. But, the output generally was poor. The advent of Medunsa held promise and certainly, a diversity of specialist began to trickle slowly, with the University of Natal following. There were many theories and speculations about this deficiency. In the medical subspecialties, such products were a rare breed. I found one qualified cardiologist at Medunsa, Dr T J Mariba. When I retired, there was one cardiologist and two others in training. Subsequently, University of Cape Town, joined in the production of at least one other African cardiologist. Post independence, a gratifying pace all round, for the training of Physicians picked up in the country.

Staff photo on retirement

I had the privilege post independence also to serve in the predominantly white bodies such as the Interim Medical Council, the Moodley Commission on Academic Health Centres. I was appointed chairperson of the first EDL committee, literally drafting the first edition alone when the academics and various sceptics stalled. I also had the honour to chair the committee that compiled the PMB lists for the Medical Schemes Act, being a member of the Hoffenberg Committee on postgraduate medical education. This committee devised the new internship training rules and introduced compulsory community service for doctors.

I suspected that Minister Nkosazana Dlamini-Zuma's advisors honoured me with these pioneering roles as the readily available senior specialist African who could be trusted politically. On some issues, it was not as we proposed. For example, introduction of community service for trainee registrars was vehemently opposed by the academics, and was stalled permanently. The only political opposition to our suggestions, was on the closure of the Transkei medical faculty. This surprised us, as besides this facility being a relic of a Bantustan system, it had very genuine serious academic problems at the time.

Other accolades included being a member of the ministerial committee on organ transplant, a member of the committee to evaluate legislation on introducing possible euthanasia. Moving on this later part of the road to somewhere, almost at the sunset of my life was politically fulfilling. I happily led the team to Cuba twice, at the beginning of the system to recruit doctors. The highlight was my shaking hands with Fidel Castro, as well as sampling the Cuban system of health care delivery, as well as admiring the seemingly too egalitarian but compact Cuban socio-political life.

At home, my sunset joyful roles included serving in the SAMA Research and Ethics Committee, and by now I had maintained some stamina to publish albeit under difficult circumstances.

IT IS SUNSET AT LAST

The top of the socio-medical ladder had been unobtrusively reached. It had been an unplanned journey all the way, but fulfilling in the end. I round off my destination at somewhere as a co-architect in the development of the new health system in a free South Africa in one's life time. I bowed out of Medunsa in 1998, a year beyond the compulsory period of retirement. I had nursed a little hope of continuing a little longer, even on the very fringe, especially that my health held out so superbly well.

In general, I did not feel like I was in a perpetual battle or struggling to move in whatever direction I now faced. I next smoothly found a slot at the Gauteng department of health as one of the advisors to Dr Gwen Ramokgopa, the MEC. It was at the time that HIV was on the door step of the country. My role was on broad administrative issues and travelling to various hospitals to collect data first hand. After a fruitful and enjoyable two years, I returned to clinical medical practice. I was appointed Senior Specialist in Internal medicine, first at Natalspruit hospital, then Tembisa hospital. At this stage I also accepted a part time post as lecturer to post-graduate students in cardiology in Family Medicine under Professor Sam Mhlongo at Medunsa. I was a bit of a rolling stone, but comfortable. The law did not allow that I be given a position higher than Senior Specialist in the province where I had been Professor and Principal Specialist. But, I was happy with the quasi-demotion.

Next I moved into private cardiological practice at Sunninghill hospital plus taking up a part time position in the cardiology section at Military 1 hospital. I also opened rooms at Aarwyp private hospital, after a brief spell at sunward clinic at Boksburg. With a bit of appropriate foot work, after quite a spell, I plunged joyfully into interventional cardiology.

Mokhobo and Colleagues at year function Potchefstroom Hospital

I was showered with age related honours! The Medical Association and Colleges of Medicine made me a life time member. The Colleges of Medicine also recognised my contribution to the development of the new health service, in the realm of drug policy development and especially the Essential Drug List philosophy.

I have arrived, so to speak, I am somewhere from nowhere indeed. I retired formally from centre stage medical and cardiac practice and relocated to my home town Potchefstroom in 2007. But, the bug was still biting and my health remains superb. So I took a post on a temporary permanent basis, renewable annually as Principal Specialist/Cardiologist at the provincial hospital.

THIS IS THE JOURNEY

The pregnancy of the boy was probably unplanned. By luck the birth was conducted without mishap by a family untrained traditional midwife. If the adopting father had not died that young, the young Kubedi would ended being a farm worker for life. His seeming good qualities would have seen him ascending the leadership ladder at Von Abo's as foreman, tractor driver and possibly a priest of his church. He bears no Christian name as is commonly the practice. His senior clan name would have made him a revered elder as he aged. Nobody knows where and how his grandfather got a Irish name.

Starting school was a mere formality to give the farm dwellers children at least four years for minimum functional literacy. When Patrick continued with school from nearby Mooibank plot, it was a mere formality also. The plot owner had only two African families working for him. There was no need for extra farm hands, except as replacement for an adult that dies. The plot was small.

THE SOCIAL ASPECT, A BIT OF DERAILMENT

The nowhere man went into self imposed exile with a wife and three children. Swaziland provided the ideal environment to give our children the best, away from the rippling of Bantu Education. Ironically, in Daveyton, though, became necessary to be involved in the system so to speak. The community demanded and expected. The one advantage of this collaboration was that I got my children into school younger than the age prescribed for Africans. Lesotho also provided a safe haven and facilitated the process to obtain scholarships for two of my children, both of whom studied at universities outside South Africa. One completed his first degree at the National University of Lesotho (NUL). My daughter went to Zambia and the United Kingdom for further study, whilst my eldest son sampled the life at NUL, Swaziland campus and Botswana campus. The former University of Botswana, Lesotho and Swaziland (UBLS) had been split into three independent campuses.

My professional wife remained unemployed and full time housewife. In 1973, I left her alone for the best part of a year. I reached a stage where I now had to think of the future in terms of both financial ability or pension and seriously consider where my permanent home will be. As a contract worker, one could not save for a pension and my income in Lesotho compared to the salaries in South Africa, was too little. After much family discussions, the first marriage collapsed for obvious various factors. Even after Medunsa rejected my first application for lack of Bantu Specialist post, I accepted Chief Mangope's bait and left for Bophutatswana, where for a few years I cohabitted with another professional woman. Interestingly, she was also a social worker and a divorcee. As a VIP guest in Swaziland, I had attended the latter woman's wedding. She relocated to Bophutatswana, found a job easily and was with me as I languished first in the primitive village of Lomanyaneng and for a brief stay in the garage at the South African Commissioner's place. I subsequently legalised our relationship and got our two daughters retrospectively be in wedlock children. Dawn, my second wife was not totally sold to the Bophutatswana life, despite the relative comfort. Fortunately she had lots of company in the half hearted acceptance of an independent state. Mangope was aware of her attitude, and there was no love lost between the two. She was not like other ministers' wives. She was popular outside Bophutatswana, had several friends and contacts. So when we had to relocate to Johannesburg, as I took the Medunsa job, she had no difficulty finding a lucrative job at Eskom.

For one thing the basic education for our daughters in Bophutatswana was excellent. Our second daughter, however, continued at St Mary's school for girls to finish matriculation, whilst her sister went to the University of Cape Town. Her younger sister followed later at the same University. We could afford it. Our move to Johannesburg coincided with the release of Mr Mandela and the historic events leading to proper independence. My wife had the honour of serving in the first Independent Electoral Commission.

Towards the sunset stage, when my daughters had completed their university studies, a third derailment step in my social life occurred. We divorced and for a while I was a bachelor. This was the time after retirement from Medunsa. I moved to Potchefstroom, my home town, in semi-retirement with my third wife. I had met this lady in church.

Mokhobo+third (present) wife, Mokhobo at present hospital,
retired working part time, picture at year end function

She is not professional and is very happy as a full time house wife.
On the other hand, I am enjoying being pampered and mothered for
the first time. Somehow, in my old age, I now for the first time feel how
maternal pampering feels like.

The life in Potchefstroom cannot be described as spectacular.

THE CHURCH LIFE NOW AND PAST

Mokhobo, second wife with Bishop Ming and his wife, A M E Church head.

Throughout my peregrinations, I have been deeply involved in the church. I have worked with older pastors in my younger days and now work with younger pastors in my old age. The church culture has changed over the years also. The pastors of today are more educated. In the olden days, with older and less educated pastors, there were frequent clashes, especially with lay members of one organisation, the Lay Organisation. I had occasion to witness the pastors of olden days mix tradition with Christian religion. This happened at the time of appointments, when these gentlemen would believe that African muti would influence a bishop in his godly decisions about appointments. I have served in many roles, at times I would serve in more than one role. I am not sure, however, if the educated pastors of today read the bible with the same open-mindedness as I do. I have also delved deeply into the history of the Christian movement and the compilation of the holy bible, but remain a committed Christian. I have not been able to impart the same passion on the Christian religion to any of my five children.

Very few of the land marks of the old location are recognisable. One only treasures memories of what could have been where. The church, the school and my uncle's hovel as well as my room at the Sepotokeles, exist only in memory. I have fond memories of the mission house, where on Sundays, I would be invited for a sumptuous meal after church. The beetroot on the plate was a delicacy and novelty I enjoyed, as I had not seen this "red" vegetable in my younger farm life. I believe such occasional good meals, such as also obtain at funerals and weddings, did much to prevent florid malnutrition. The food at Mooibank was bare as regards nutritive value. This place, my home, is totally not recognisable to me also.

POTCHEFSTROOM, 2012 AND MAYBE TOMORROW

I have come full circle on a road essentially unplanned and not charted in any way. Old age is creeping in. One's social life outside the church offers little. But the church also lacks certain elements of a happy childhood life. On Sunday mornings, the tolling of the bells in a musical staccato, are missing. At my church, not only has the modern life removed the Sunday morning tolls, but that bell ring at the funeral services is no more. It used to have a distinctive emotive effect, endorsing an appropriate sombre mood.

My contemporaries are no more, most of the ones I would recognise. The intermediate age groups and some younger ones know something about me. The high school fame and Mr Calderbank's gesture seemed to have reverberated for some time after I left home. However, socialising is at a minimum level, sometimes bordering on loneliness. There is one contemporary, a golfing mate with whom I enjoy a round of golf. My competitive spirit in golf remains high, so I have joined a society of young and middle aged health workers, mostly doctors. I also join some competitions run by the local club. This is the country club where I used to caddy. The lay out of the course has changed markedly. There are photographs showing past events. When I look at these pictures, I vividly remember how black caddies were treated with much denigration. For one thing, the club house was out of bounds completely, and you were regarded always as a potential thief. You got your fee of either nine pence for nine holes or one shilling and six pence for eighteen holes, and left.

There was no food nor refreshments. The gambling afterwards among caddies, in some street corner in the township was always an uplifting pastime. Even the occasional fights over gambling issues provided a worth while distraction after golf recreation.

The contract job at the local provincial hospital is an absolute pleasure. I have had this renewed annually for the past five years. It is hard to bravely take a decision for formal retirement once and for all. Every year when the time for renewing arrives, hesitancy and near fear of the unknown takes the upper hand. I appreciate the accolades one receives for teaching the modern day young graduates. But my view is that learning is a life long process and this process is a two way interaction. Many things have changed since my time. There is also the tendency to forget issues you do not meet often. I learn a lot from the cadres of junior doctors who come through my medical department. I have to read journals in order to keep breast and also to collect points to remain on the Health Profession's register.

The patients are generous with humbling words of gratitude, even when nature has done the healing. More humbling is when you are thanked for having tried your best but lost the battle and the patient has died. The patients include all races, the majority among whites are white Afrikaners. At this stage, I have forgotten the denigrating Wits experience. I have come to appreciate that human beings are all the same. If left to make their choices for what they believe to be a good doctor, ethnicity plays no part. Also, our patients, regardless of ethnicity, have blind faith in every doctor and are often too gullible most of them. The work is challenging, especially as there is a tinge of déjà vu. This level two hospital is markedly under-resourced. The clientele emanates from the poor third world South African populace, and this applies to all racial groups.

My superb health and perpetual youthfulness have accompanied me back home. The atmosphere at the hospital is congenial, my immediate neighbours all round are Afrikaans speaking. Where the fencing wall is low enough we greet and talk, but there has never been any close social interaction. It is by surprise that I got a house where the old location of Makweteng was. Hence, the residents of this suburb are descendents of the so-called poor whites, who lived with the Africans and Indian people in years gone by. The Africans were removed to the other side of town, adjacent to the industrial areas, whilst Indians and "Coloureds", were relocated further away in separated areas. The political reasons were to prevent interracial mixing, or possible intermarriage. Such happenings would be a serious breach of the sacred apartheid philosophy and practice. In time, the apartheid boundaries have crumbled. Initially segregated areas, are occupied and integrated through social circumstances. Even the previously pure racial cemeteries are integrated. The township schools though, are only for non-whites, especially Africans and coloureds. The former white schools are completely mixed. My five children from the two previous marriages are prospering in the new democratic state. They are in the big city of Johannesburg. None of them ventured into medicine as a profession. There are currently nine grand children and four great grand children. At least one grand daughter is passionate about becoming a medical doctor.

The nowhere has become a pleasant some destination. Indeed one piccanin or kaffertjie has arrived, after a fulfilling though uncharted uncertain road of life.

THE QUESTION OF A LEGACY

This is a very difficult aspect of the journey and the destination or destiny for that matter. Whenever one visits any of the southern African states, one gets embarrassed to realise how people will remember the so-called wonderful excellent performance of decades ago. It is the same experience with Mahikeng, Daveyton and the East Rand as well as the West Rand. These disarming kind accolades are not tangible or visible legacies. They are not monuments nor permanent historical sign posts.

A legacy will probably be in the thoughts and sentiments of my students, some of my colleagues, fellow church members, and a number of friends who will outlive me. Many of my relatives will also be a reservoir of memories in many forms. For me, it is mission accomplished, an unplanned journey is complete and I bow out with pride and satisfaction.

Printed in Great Britain
by Amazon

87373443R00058